ISS  I0052035

Dediu Newsletter

Author: Michael M. Dediu

Monthly news, reviews, comments and suggestions for a better and wiser world

---

Vol. 2, Nr. 11 (23), 6 October 2018

DERC Publishing House

Tewksbury (Boston), Massachusetts, U. S. A.

For subscriptions please use the contact form at www.derc.com

Published and printed in the
United States of America
On the Great Seal of the United States are included:
E Pluribus Unum (Out of many, one)
Annuit Coeptis (He has approved of the undertakings)
Novus Ordo Seclorum (New order of the ages)

Dediu, Michael M.

Dediu Newsletter Vol 2, Number 11 (23), 6 October 2018
Monthly reviews, comments and suggestions for a better and wiser world

ISSN 2475-2061
ISBN 978-1-939757-76-0

Preface

September 2018 was nice and warm, a pleasant end of summer, with preparations for the starting of school.

Many good news from research in science, medicine, technology, and other areas. On 7th of September we had the National Grateful Patient Day: spreading gratitude and hope by thanking the doctors, nurses and their assistants who help the patients. Also, Jeff Bezos' Blue Origin space transport company has won a contract to supply engines for the massive Vulcan rocket built by United Launch Alliance, the joint venture between Boeing and Lockheed Martin. And researchers work on a project to develop artificial intelligence, machine autonomy, and cyber security programs for a future constellation of low-cost satellites operating in low-Earth orbit.

In this 11th newsletter of the second volume, the 23rd in total, we included the most relevant news, in a balanced approach, usually directly from the source, to help the general public better understand the realities around us. We included also several nice photos - I thank my wife for her photo assistance. Being well and correctly informed is a sine qua non requirement for everybody, in order to make the right decisions for the future.

Enjoy this newsletter and be optimist!

Michael M. Dediu, Ph. D.

Tewksbury (Boston), U. S. A., 6 October 2018

USA, the University of California, Berkeley (1868, named after the philosopher and mathematician Bishop George Berkeley (1685-1753), motto Fiat lux (Let there be light), 36,200 students, 72 Nobel laureates, 500 ha campus), Physics Department in Le Conte Hall (1924, center), Campanile (back (61 bells (full concert carillon) and clock tower). 1914, 94 m, 7 floors, observation deck on the 8th floor, inspired by il Campanile (850, 1514, 1912, 99 m) di San Marco (1084), Venezia (421, Venice), Italy (900 BC)).

Table of Contents

Japan, Osaka (which means "large hill" or "large slope", in 645 capital, 400 km west of Tokyo, the second largest city after Tokyo, metropolitan area around has 19,000,000 people, along with Paris and London is one of the most productive city in the world with a GDP of $341 billions, situated at the mouth of the Yodo River on Osaka Bay of the Pacific Ocean), a small Buddhist Temple west of Shin Osaka Washington Plaza Hotel and southwest of Shin Osaka Station (1964, 2011, 3 km from the older Osaka Station).

United States of America

(Population 324.4 M, rank 3, growth 0.7%. Free: 89 of 100).
Reports: If stacked one on top of another, all the pages of regulations handed down by the federal bureaucracy would slightly dwarf the Torre di Pisa (Leaning Tower of Pisa in Italy, which is the campanile of the Cathedral of Pisa, Tower started 845 years ago, on August 14, 1173, height 55.86 m). These stifling regulations have caused uncertainty, abuses, loses of over $100 B, and instability in the U.S.

Reports: GOP leaders in Congress have completely failed to do what they said they would do. As candidates, begging to be re-elected, they campaigned as conservatives, yet, after winning, they went back to their old ways, and legislated as liberals. The grass roots were told that once Republicans controlled the House, then it was the Senate, and most recently the White House; it was only then that they would be able to enact real conservative policies. Well, that has happened, and voters are still waiting. Washington needs leaders who honor their oath to support and defend the Constitution, and who will not hand our country over to the liberals. It's time for leaders in Washington to keep their promises and fulfill their commitments to taxpayers.

12 September 2018. Reports: More than 60 U.S. industry groups - ranging from retailing, toy manufacturing, farming and tech - will launch a coalition today, called Americans for Free Trade, taking the fight public over billions of dollars of U.S. tariffs. The U.S. Chamber of Commerce, the National Association of Manufacturers, the Business Roundtable, and Koch brothers are running separate lobbying efforts to promote free trade.

The company Takeda will be moving its U.S. Headquarters from Chicago area to Boston.

A Redwood City, CA, based company said that private information from about 1,100 people was exposed due to a cybersecurity attack.

14 September 2018. Reports: Dozens of gas explosions killed at least one person, injured 12 more, and forced thousands to evacuate from three communities north of Boston. Some 70 fires, explosions or investigations of gas odor were reported, according to Massachusetts State Police. NiSource's Columbia Gas unit had said earlier that it would be upgrading gas lines in neighborhoods across the state.

Reports: Median U.S. household income reached $61,400 last year, according to Census Bureau figures announced Wednesday, 12 Sep. That is the highest level ever.

Reports: K-12 Tax & Spending: Golden retirement — seven ex-Milwaukee County prosecutors get $1 million-plus cash payouts, while college tuition is up 191%.

Reports: In May, a group of 16 Republican senators came together to say we were willing to work nights, weekends, and through the annual August recess to deliver results, specifically on confirmations and funding. This additional time created an opportunity for Congress to fully fund the government on time for the first time in 22 years. Despite some progress, in typical Washington fashion, Congress has again found a way to fall short of fulfilling its constitutional responsibility. There is still time before the end of the fiscal year on Sept. 30, but Congress has thrown in the towel. It has turned to another continuing resolution to keep the lights on until December. This is completely unacceptable.
Another funding failure further exposes the underlying problems with the funding process used by Congress since 1974. It has only fully funded the government four times in the past 44 years. It has locked Washington in a cycle of continuing resolutions, and last-minute spending deals. To be successful, this new funding process needs to include specific milestones for completing funding, and appropriate consequences if Congress fails to meet those markers.

Reports: As of August, eight of the 10 government biggest spenders had worked through less than 40% of their budgets, or roughly just $240 B of more than $1 trillion. And because spending caps were lifted, even more money needs to go out the door. And no one wants to spend everything early on, or they could end up short. Last year, the Pentagon dropped $50 B in the last week of September, around five times what they burn through in a normal week. They bought furniture and computers.

Reports: The harsh truth about some big spender cities; Madison's long term, disastrous reading results.

Wealthy L.A. schools' vaccination rates are as low as South Sudan's.

About 40% of economics experiments fail replication survey.

Colleges teach students to see bias where it doesn't exist.

California's poverty rate is still the highest in the nation.

A recent study finds that the tool most often used to assess the efficiency of nonprofit organizations isn't just inaccurate – it can actually be negatively correlated with efficiency. – North Carolina State University, Nonprofit Management & Leadership, Sept-2018

24 September 2018. Reports: The latest tariffs spare many high-profile consumer technology items, such as smartwatches and speakers, but not so the less flashy home modems, routers and switching and networking gear, that make them work. The basic gear that keeps the internet functioning was not included in a newly created U.S. tariff code that was exempted from the latest China tariffs, according to the U.S. Customs and Border Protection Agency. The move effectively creates a two-tiered tariff structure for consumer internet, with products such as Apple's watch, Amazon's Echo smart speaker and Fitbit's fitness tracker favored over routers and internet gateways from Arris, Netgear, D-Link and others.

U.S. airlines' revenue from baggage and reservation change fees rose to $7.5 B in 2017 from $5.7 B in 2010. Just last week, American Airlines became the latest major airline to raise fees for checked bags by $5 for the first bag to $30, joining Delta, United and JetBlue. Congress is set to vote on the measure this week, ahead of a September 30 deadline.

25 September 2018. Reports: Last year the President made one of the policy mistakes of his young presidency by failing to veto the $1.3 trillion omnibus spending bill. One of the Republican Congress' biggest mistakes was sending him that bloated appropriations bill in the first place. It has only demoralized the Republican voters — the same group that hasn't been showing up in special election races this year. In a few weeks Congress will again send to the White House a near $1 trillion bill, that perpetuates the billions of dollars of deficit spending each day. If this stands and the President signs the bill, kiss the Republican House goodbye, and probably the Senate, too. When Republicans act and spend like Democrats, they lose.

Reports: Tax cuts are not driving federal deficits upward. It's just a way for lawmakers to distract the public, while they crank up the spending machine. Just like the Senate did this week. Through August, the federal deficit topped $898 B. Over the same period last year, the deficit was $674 B. So, the deficit is running $224 B higher this fiscal year, compared with last. But the Treasury data also show that federal revenues through August totaled $2.985 T. That's an increase of $19 B over the previous year. In other words, despite the tax cuts, federal revenues are running higher this year than last.

Reports: This year, total health care spending will increase 5.3%, according to a recent estimate from the Centers for Medicare and Medicaid Services. That's after spending rose by 4.6% last year to total $3.5 T.

Dr. Newt Gingrich: For more than 60 years, liberals have been able to rely on a left-leaning Supreme Court to impose radical values on America. For six decades, lawyers have dominated the American people, and changed policies by judicial fiat, which they could not otherwise get passed through the political process involving American voters.

Reports: There is a big problem: Congress' failure to curtail spending. Polls taken in 2016 showed the public perceived that government wasted about half the money it collected. Congress and the administration can do a lot more to get our fiscal house in order. One common-sense fix, that has been neglected, is confronting the irrational use-it-or-lose budget practices in Washington. In the private economy, any business, that spends less on overhead than budgeted, is rewarded. In government, the opposite is true. Agencies that spend less than they received are punished, in their view, with lower budgets. Rather than lock in these savings, agencies engage in end-of-the-fiscal-year spending sprees.

Reports: The last decade (1 Jan 1991 – 31 Dec 2000) of the 20th Century (1 Jan 1901 – 31 Dec 2000) brought waves of change to the U.S. military after the Berlin Wall came down in 1989, and Russia abandoned Communism, when Pentagon leaders adjusted to a post-Soviet world, and the end of the Cold War. People hoped for peace and less military expenses.

Reports: If there's something the government does well, it's spend money. It does it with great fervor, no matter who's in charge of Congress or the White House. And it's made easier these days, thanks to our legislators' collective unwillingness to follow a regular budget process and their carelessness about the fiscal health of this country. Case in point: the $854 B Senate spending bill making its way to the House this last week of September.
Considering how large the total spending package is, you'd think it might pay for all discretionary spending (that's the part of the budget that funds transportation, defense, infrastructure, education, and more). But it's only a little more than 65% of discretionary spending for 2019. It covers just one year of defense spending (a Republican priority) and the Labor, Health and Human Services and Education bill (a Democratic one). As for the remaining discretionary spending, it's provided in a smaller bill meant to fund the government through Dec. 7.
The best way to describe the funding vehicle is as a political balancing act that allows Congress to, yet again, fail to deliver on its No. 1 job: passing an annual spending bill on time.
Congress abandons its responsibility for reducing regulations, by creating more airline regulation, with regards to the size of airline seats.

Reports: Harvard raised $9.6 B in its latest campaign, but IQ scores are on the decline.

Reports: The CBO forecast in 2017 that over the next decade the national debt will double to 150% of GDP in about 20 years. Those are debt numbers that don't have a happy ending — just ask the citizens of Puerto Rico, Detroit, and Greece.

Reports: An Air Force squadron spent almost $56,000 on dozens of metal coffee cups, and their replacements, over the past three years, in the latest example Pentagon procurement pricing irregularities. "It's always important to think about the problem that any piece of equipment is intended to solve," Dan Grazier, of Project On Government Oversight, a government watchdog, told Fox News Tuesday, 2 October, 2018. "If this cup is only meant to heat water for coffee or tea, then its purpose is to aid in the crew's alertness by providing caffeine. The exact same effect can be achieved with a few cans of Red Bull which would be far less expensive." Grazier, who served in the Marines, added: "Lest anyone shrug this example of waste off as minor, considering the billions of dollars wasted by the government, the thousands of dollars wasted here, combined with a few thousand dollars in a million other examples, add up to the billions in waste.

Reports: The U.S. federal debt increased by $1.27 T in fiscal 2018 - which runs from October 1 through September 30 - according to data released by the Treasury. The figure marks the eighth fiscal year, in the last eleven, in which the debt increased by at least one trillion dollars, and was the sixth largest fiscal-year debt increase in U.S. history. The national debt now totals $21.51 T.

Puerto Rico: (Population 3.6 M, rank 134, decrease 0.1%; an unincorporated territory of the United States, located in the northeast Caribbean Sea, 1,600 km southeast of Miami, Florida.).

United Nations.   There are 195 officially recognized countries. Around 44,000 people work for the United Nations. There is a wide range of jobs: Researchers, IT-specialists, lawyers, experts on finance and administration, or translators work at the New York headquarters, at the official locations, or at specialized agencies. More than half of the UN's workforce is employed in the field, in projects of humanitarian aid, or on peace missions.

21 September 2018. Reports: Some world leaders are gathering at the United Nations for the 73rd annual U.N. General Assembly in New York City.

USA, Tewksbury (settled 1637, incorporated 1734, named after Tewkesbury, England, 31 km northwest of Boston): a golf course.

China, Japan, and neighbors

China: (Population 1.4 B, rank 1, growth 0.4%. Freedom House reports for 2018: Not Free (15 of 100)). Reports: China is in a race for counter-drone technology and laser weapons, as it tries to catch up with U.S.

7 September 2018. Xinhua: China expressed strong dissatisfaction on Thursday, 6 Sep, after a naval vessel from the United Kingdom sailed into territorial waters off China's Xisha Islands, with China urging an immediate cessation of such provocative actions. Reuters reported that HMS Albion, a 22,000-ton amphibious warship, passed near the Xisha Islands on August 31, on its way to Vietnam.

"HMS Albion exercised her rights for freedom of navigation in full compliance with international law and norms," Reuters cited a spokesman for the Royal Navy as saying.

The warship illegally entered territorial waters without permission from the Chinese government, and China's Navy, a branch of the People's Liberation Army, verified and identified the warship in accordance with law, and warned it to leave, a Foreign Ministry (FM) representative said at a daily news briefing.

The Xisha Islands are an inherent territory of China, FM said. "The action taken by the British ship violated Chinese law and relevant international law, and infringed on China's sovereignty," and China strongly protests such moves and has lodged solemn representations, FM added.

China urged the UK to immediately stop such provocations to avoid harming overall bilateral relations as well as regional peace and stability, FM added.

Also, on Thursday, a Ministry of National Defense (MND) spokesman said that such an action undermines China's sovereignty and security interests, and can easily lead to accidents in the air and on the sea. MND noted that the situation in the South China Sea is becoming better thanks to the efforts made by China and members of the Association of Southeast Asian Nations.

However, some countries outside the region ignore this positive trend, dispatch planes and ships to stir up trouble in the region and disturb peace and security, MND said, adding that the Chinese military will take all necessary measures to resolutely defend national security and sovereignty.

Reports: America's elite universities are censoring themselves on China.

Chinese University hires 'Patriotic,' 'Politically Educated' mentors for foreign students.

World's leading Human Rights Groups tell Google to cancel its China censorship plan.

10 September 2018. Reports: China's trade surplus with the U.S. in August reached a record $31.1 B despite exports climbing at the slowest pace since March. Shipments were up 9.8% and imports up 20%. The U.S. has imposed $50 B in duties against China, with another $200 B in the works, and an extra $267 B in tariffs proposed.

Reports: China celebrates Confucius (551 BC - 479 BC, aged 72), Chinese teacher, editor, politician, and philosopher of the Spring and Autumn Period of Chinese history.

11 September 2018. Reports: China will ask the World Trade Organization to impose sanctions on the U.S. next week, for non-compliance related to a ruling regarding U.S. dumping duties. The 2017 WTO ruling was related to several industries ranging from machinery to metals to light industry, for a total annual export value of up to $8.4B.

14 September 2018. Reports: Following many rumors, 16 bipartisan members of the U.S. House of Representatives have asked Google if it will re-enter the Chinese search engine market, and if it would comply with local censorship policies upon its return. While the tech giant didn't comment, discontent over the controversial effort is circulating at the company. Seven Google employees have reportedly quit their jobs over the endeavor that's codenamed Dragonfly.

Reports: Google has been quietly collaborating with the Chinese government on a new, censored search engine — and abandoning its own ideals in the process. Because of this, senior Google scientist resigns, mentioning "Forfeiture of our values" in China.

Reports: China will not be content to only play defense in an escalating trade war with the U.S., according to the Global Times, which is published by the ruling Communist Party's People's Daily. Besides retaliating with tariffs, China could also restrict export of goods, raw materials and components core to U.S. manufacturing supply chains, former finance minister Lou Jiwei told a forum on Sunday, 16 Sep. There are also worries Beijing may be plotting a currency devaluation.

Reports: Trouble may be brewing as China's monopoly of the critical materials needed for electric vehicles and national security may be impossible to break.

18 September 2018. Reports: China has no choice but to retaliate against the latest round of U.S. tariffs, the country's Commerce Ministry said, as Vice Premier Liu He convened a meeting in Beijing to discuss the government's response.

History Report: Before the Chinese Communist Party took power, China had a chance for democracy, similar with what Taiwan, Japan and South Korea have now. Today Communist China is a force on the global stage, but remains connected to its Communist past. The grand strategies were pursued by China's paramount leaders: Mao Zedong (26 Dec 1893 – 9 Sep 1976, aged 82.7, Chairman for 27 years: 1949 – 1976), who, at the request of Stalin (18 Dec 1878 – 5 March 1953, aged 74.2, Dictator for 30 years: 1923 – 1953) and with Stalin's considerable support, unified the country and kept it whole; Deng Xiaoping (22 Aug 1904 – 19 Feb 1997, aged 92.4, Leader for 11 years: 1978 – 1989), who dragged that country into the modern world; Jiang Zemin (17 Aug 1926 – now 92.1 years, Leader for14 years: 1989 – 2003), and Hu Jintao (21 Dec 1942 – now 75.7 years old, President for 10 years: 2003 – 2013), cautious custodians of Deng's legacy; and the powerful, insecure Xi Jinping (15 June 1953 – now 65.2, President for 5.5 years: 14 March 2013 – now). Despite heavy costs, China's grand strategies have been largely successful. But success brings significant challenges — ones ever more pressing now and in the next years.

18 September 2018. Vladimir Putin met in Kremlin with First Vice Premier of the State Council of China, Han Zheng.

19 September 2018. Reports: Interest rates are important, as the China-U.S. trade battle ratchets up. Some analysts think the recent selloff in the bond market could be partially tied to concerns that China could use other measures to retaliate against the U.S. With Beijing seen as having limited room to match tariffs over the long term, some say China could attempt to dump the bonds to drive

up borrowing costs in the U.S. The 10-year Treasury yield currently stands at 3.059%.

19 September 2018. Reports: Alibaba announced at an event in Hangzhou that it plans to set up a new chip subsidiary to make customized artificial intelligence chips and embedded processors for the cloud and Internet of Things businesses. The company hopes to launch its first self-developed AI inference chip out of the Alibaba DAMO Academy in the second half of 2019. The new chip could be used for autonomous driving, smart cities and logistics. R&D spending at Alibaba is projected to double to $15 B over the next three years.

Reports: The Beidou Navigation Satellite System is a global navigation satellite system developed by China.

The Long March rocket series have been launched 284 times, sending more than 400 spacecraft into space.

21 September 2018. Xinhua: Xi Jinping, general secretary of the Central Committee of the Communist Party of China (CPC), called for focusing reforms on solving practical problems, on Thursday, 20 Sep. Xi, also Chinese president and chairman of the Central Military Commission, made the remarks while presiding over the fourth meeting of the central committee for deepening overall reform, which he heads. Both the importance and difficulty of reform lie in implementation, Xi said.

Saying that there are more and more favorable conditions for carrying out reforms and focusing on implementation, he called for putting more energy and efforts into implementation, and focusing reforms on solving real problems.

Li Keqiang and Wang Huning, both members of the Standing Committee of the Political Bureau of the CPC Central Committee, and deputy heads of the reform committee, attended the meeting.

The meeting approved a number of documents:

-- a document on promoting high-quality development;

-- a document on establishing more effective mechanisms for coordinated regional development;

-- measures on supporting pilot free trade zones' efforts to deepen reform and innovation;

-- a guideline on improving regulation of systematically important financial institutions;

-- a document on reforming and improving the national vaccine regulation system;

-- a document on integrating systems of planning, to make national development plans play a better role of strategic guidance;

-- a document on promoting the alignment of small farmers with the development of modern agriculture.

More efforts should be made to formulate policies that promote high-quality development in important areas, including manufacturing, high-tech industries, service and infrastructure, and public services, and to put protecting the people's interests at a more prominent position, said a statement released after the meeting.

More effective mechanisms for coordinated regional development should be set up by sticking to the new development philosophy, giving play to comparative advantages of each area, and narrowing regional development gap, said the statement,

Pilot free trade zones should be granted more power to reform and further open up, as well as policy support to create a good environment for investment, boost trade facilitation, and make financial innovation serve the real economy, said the statement.

Policies should be clarified to put in place institutional arrangements for identifying, regulating and dealing with systematically important financial institutions, it said.

On vaccine regulation, strong measures should be adopted to enforce strict market access, strengthen market supervision, improve logistics and delivery, standardize vaccination management, eradicate regulation loopholes, and crack down on acts violating laws and regulations, it said.

More efforts should also be made to set up a policy system supporting small farmers' development, boost their level of organization, and improve their production and operation capabilities, to transform them from traditional small farmers into modern ones, according to the statement.

23 September 2018. Xinhua. Chinese President Xi Jinping has congratulated Chinese farmers for their first harvest festival.

Xi, also general secretary of the Central Committee of the Communist Party of China (CPC) and chairman of the Central Military Commission, sent greetings and good wishes to the country's farmers on behalf of the CPC Central Committee ahead of the festival, which falls on Sept. 23, the Autumnal Equinox of this year. The CPC Central Committee's decision to create the Chinese farmers' harvest festival further demonstrates that work related to agriculture, rural areas and farmers is a top priority and holds a fundamental position, Xi noted, calling the creation of the festival "an event with profound and far-reaching influence."

"China is a large agricultural country. Priority on agriculture is the foundation and essential for the rule of the country and the people's security," Xi said. Chinese farmers have made great contributions throughout the country's history, he said, noting that historic achievements and reforms have been made in agricultural and rural development over the past four decades of rural reform.

Xi called on the country's farmers and all sectors of society to vigorously participate in the festive events and foster a good environment for the development of agriculture and rural areas as well as the wellbeing of farmers.

He also urged moves to stimulate farmers' enthusiasm, initiative and creativity so as to fully implement the rural vitalization strategy, win the tough battle against poverty and accelerate the modernization of agriculture and rural areas.

23 September 2018. Xinhua. China's Central Military Commission (CMC) on Saturday, 22 Sep, lodged solemn representations and protests against sanctions imposed by the United States.

Huang Xueping, deputy head of the CMC's office for international military cooperation, summoned the acting defense attaché at the U.S. Embassy Saturday evening, according to a CMC press release. The U.S. State Department announced Thursday, 20 Sep, that it would impose sanctions on the Equipment Development Department of the CMC and the department's director, alleging that China had violated the "Countering America's Adversaries Through Sanctions Act." Huang said the military cooperation between China and Russia is normal cooperation between sovereign states that goes in line with international law.

He called the U.S. side's unreasonable move "a flagrant breach of basic rules of international relations" and "a stark show of hegemonism" that severely harmed relations between China and the United States, as well as the two countries' militaries.

China resolutely opposes the U.S. move and will never accept it, Huang said. He said China will immediately recall the Chinese navy commander Shen Jinlong who is in the United States attending the 23rd International Sea power Symposium, and postpone the second meeting of a communication mechanism for the joint staff departments of China and the United States, scheduled for Sept. 25-27 in Beijing.

China demands the U.S. side to immediately correct its wrongdoing and withdraw the so-called sanctions. "The Chinese military reserves the right to take further countermeasures," Huang said.

Reports: Google China prototype links searches to phone numbers.

In Xi We Trust: how propaganda might be working in the New Era.

China removes unapproved, foreign content from school textbooks.

Google suppresses memo revealing plans to closely track search users in China.

China is buying African media's silence.

There are at least 48 ways to get sent to a Chinese concentration camp.

China is building a digital dictatorship to exert control over its 1.4 billion citizens. For some, "social credit" will bring privileges — for others, punishment.

Ngar Min Swe was given 7 years prison for a Facebook post.

Google is working with China, while canceling contracts with the U.S military.

History: Sino-Soviet split from 1959 (which started after the death of Stalin in 1953), shown visible cracks in the Sino-Soviet alliance. In 1973 China's foreign policy changed from an "alliance with the Soviet Union to oppose the United States" to "aligning with the United States to oppose the Soviet Union". After1989 the situation changed again.

History: 29 September 2018 China.org.cn. The memorial ceremony for the 2,569th anniversary of the birth of Confucius (551 BC – 479 BC, aged 72) was held in the Southern Confucius Ancestral Temple in Quzhou, southeast China's Zhejiang province on Sept. 28, 2018. Kong Xiangkai, a 75th generation (33.33 years/generation) lineal descendant of Confucius, serves as the master of ceremony.

Reports: Google suppresses memo revealing plans to closely track search users in China.

Reports: China canceled a high-level annual security meeting with the U.S., planned for mid-October, saying a high-level military official wouldn't be available to meet with Defense Sec. James Mattis. Aside from ongoing trade tensions, the news follows on recent developments in the military arena, including U.S. equipment sales to Taiwan and B-52 flyovers in the East China Sea and South China Sea.

1 October 2018. Vladimir Putin sent a message of greetings to President of the People's Republic of China, Xi Jinping, on the Republic's 69th anniversary (1949).

Hong Kong. (Population 7.3 M, rank 104, growth 0.8%. Partly Free: 61 of 100).

Macau (Population 622 K, rank 167, growth 1.7 %.)

Taiwan: (Population 23.6 M, rank 56, growth 0.3%. Free, 91 of 100). Reports: Taiwan to form fleet of armed unmanned aerial vehicles (UAVs) to patrol its coastline.

17 September 2018. China Daily: Taiwan's intelligence agencies have been persuading students from the Chinese mainland, studying at universities in Taiwan, to provide confidential information to Taiwan's spy network, by offering money, relationships and sex, security authorities said.

The intelligence agencies have been targeting the mainland and recklessly stepping up information collection, and infiltration activities for some time, An Fengshan, spokesman for the Taiwan Affairs Office of the State Council, said on Sunday, 16 Sep.

"Taiwan authorities should immediately stop all espionage targeting the Chinese mainland, to prevent further damage to the increasingly complicated cross-Straits relations," he said.

To prevent such activities, which endanger the development of both cross-Straits relations, and national security, mainland security authorities recently launched an operation code-named 2018 Thunder, according to a report by China Central Television.

More than 100 Taiwan-related spy cases have been handled during the operation, including the arrest of a group of spies from Taiwan and their recruits, security authorities said. Taiwan's intelligence agencies prefer to target postgraduate or PhD exchange students with majors in politics, economics, science or military technology, because of their potential access to key information, security authorities said. The intelligence agencies have also planted a large number of agents at universities. They approach students from the mainland, and offer money for information.

In a case that was made public over the weekend, an 18-year-old exchange student from the mainland was targeted by a Taiwan spy calling herself Hsu Chia-ying, at a party in 2011. She claimed to be a couple of years older than the student and an admirer of his talent. The pair began to date, and the relationship soon turned sexual. Hsu showed great interest in the mainland student's major, which allowed contact with classified information related to national defense.

Hsu asked the student to report on what he had learned on a daily basis after he returned to the university on the mainland. She also wanted to know details about the laboratories at the university.

As a postgraduate student, the student had the opportunity to take part in projects in key State laboratories. When Hsu demanded more information, the student became suspicious. He wanted to end the relationship but Hsu objected, sending emails to his family and friends telling them that he had seduced her in Taiwan. Under pressure, the student continued to provide information to Hsu.

Hsu's activities were discovered by security authorities in 2014. Her real name is Hsu Li-ting and she is actually 16 years older than the student. She is an agent of the Taiwan Military Intelligence Bureau, the authorities said.

The authorities said that, over three years, the student provided Hsu with about 100 pieces of information on science and technology related to national defense and was paid about 45,000 yuan ($6,590). At the beginning, the Taiwan agents only ask students for nonconfidential information, such as academic documents, an officer of the Beijing State Security Bureau told CCTV, adding that they then offer money and later use the transactions to blackmail the students. They also encourage the students to become civil servants in suggested posts. Once a student reaches a key position, the agents use blackmail to get more classified information.

Intelligence agents in Taiwan have also been using local foundations, that fund students from the Chinese mainland to participate in academic exchange programs, as recruitment tools.

Efforts by Taiwan's intelligence agencies to target young people is an exploitation of the expansion of cross-Straits exchanges, security authorities said, calling the practice extremely vile.

26 September 2018. Xinhua. A spokesman for the Chinese military said Tuesday, 25 Sep, that it was strongly dissatisfied with, and resolutely opposed to planned U.S. arms sales to Taiwan.

"The Chinese military lodges solemn representations to the U.S. side over the move," said Ren Guoqiang, spokesman for China's Ministry of National Defense. Ren's comment came after the U.S. government informed congress of its decision to sell weapons worth about 330 millions of U.S. dollars to Taiwan on Tuesday.

"Taiwan is a part of China, and the one-China principle is the political foundation of China-U.S. relationship," Ren said.

"The U.S. move has severely violated the one-China principle and regulations of three Sino-U.S. Joint Communiques, interfered with China's domestic affairs, and harmed China's sovereignty and security interests, and seriously damaged China-U.S. ties, relations between the two militaries, as well as peace and stability across the Taiwan Strait.

"The Chinese military's determination and will to safeguard China's sovereignty and territorial integrity is steadfast and unshakable.

"We strongly urge the U.S. side to abide by the one-China principle, and the regulations of the three Sino-U.S. Joint Communiques, immediately revoke arms sales to Taiwan, and stop military contact with Taiwan including arms sales, so as not to further damage the China-U.S. ties, relations between the two militaries, as well as peace and stability across the Taiwan Strait."

Japan (Population 127.5 M, rank 11, decrease 0.2%. Free, 96 of 100). Reports: Lockheed Martin is working with the U.S. Air Force on F-22-F-35 hybrid fighter intended for Japan.

10 September 2018. Reports: Japan's Q2 GDP growth was the fastest since early 2016, hitting an annualized rate of 3% compared to the initial reading of 1.9%.

10 September 2018. The President of Russia and Prime Minister of Japan Shinzo Abe visited the Russian-Japanese Mazda

Sollers Manufacturing Rus engine plant in Vladivostok, and attended a ceremony launching an assembly line for the manufacture of Mazda car engines.

Vladimir Putin held talks with Prime Minister of Japan Shinzo Abe in Vladivostok. Vladimir Putin and Shinzo Abe discussed topical bilateral matters, in particular economic, humanitarian, and military cooperation.

Japan, Fuji (city 25 km south of Mount Fuji, 3776 m), on Fuji Odori - a Japanese temple with two lanterns and a nice garden.

18 September 2018. Reports: The first private passenger that will voyage around the Moon has been named as Japanese billionaire Yusaku Maezawa, the founder and CEO of online fashion retailer Zozo. He'll be riding aboard SpaceX's forthcoming Big Falcon Rocket spaceship for a flight tentatively planned for 2023. The launch is expected to take the race to commercialize space travel to new heights.

20 September 2018. Reports: Japan's Zaif is the latest crypto exchange to be attacked by cybercriminals, with losses of Bitcoin and two other digital currencies estimated at about $60 M. The

incident follows the high-profile theft by cybercriminals of $530 M earlier this year at Tokyo-based Coincheck - one of the world's biggest cybercriminals' attack.

The people ask the authorities to arrest the cybercriminals.

20 September 2018. Vladimir Putin congratulated Prime Minister of Japan, Shinzo Abe, on his re-election as the leader of the Liberal Democratic Party of Japan.

Afghanistan: (Population 35.5 M, rank 40, growth 2.5%. Not free: 24 of 100).

South Korea: (Population 50.9 M, rank 27, growth 0.4%. Free, 82 of 100). 12 September 2018. Vladimir Putin had a meeting with Prime Minister of the Republic of Korea, Lee Nak-yeon, on the sidelines of the Eastern Economic Forum in Vladivostok.

18 September 2018. Reports: South Korean President Moon Jae-in has arrived in Pyongyang for a three-day summit with Kim Jong-un, aimed at reviving inter-Korean relations, and stalled nuclear negotiations between the U.S. and North Korea. Underscoring the emphasis on trade and economic engagement, several prominent business leaders accompanied Moon, including Lee Jae-yong, the heir to the Samsung conglomerate.

North Korea: (Population 25.4 M, rank 52, growth 0.5%. Not free: 3 of 100). History: Between 1979 and 1983 North Korea saw the small Caribbean spice island of Grenada as the front line of the global struggle against US.

20 September 2018. Reports: Denuclearization negotiations with North Korea will be completed by January 2021, according to Secretary of State Mike Pompeo. "We welcome... the permanent dismantlement of all facilities at Yongbyon and the Tongchang-ri site in the presence of U.S. and international inspectors. On the basis of these important commitments, the U.S. is prepared to engage immediately in negotiations to transform U.S. - DPRK relations."

History: Both Communist China and North Korea were created by Stalin in the late 1940s, and the twists and turns in high-level diplomacy between them started then, and continued to the death of Mao Zedong in 1976. The tensions that currently plague the alliance between the two Communist countries have been present from the very beginning of the relationship.

Vietnam (Population 95.5 M, rank 15, growth 1%. Not free, 20 of 100). 6 September 2018. The President of Russia received in Sochi, Russia, General Secretary of the Communist Party of the Socialist Republic of Vietnam, Nguyen Phu Trong, who is in Russia on an official visit.

The discussion focused on major issues of Russian-Vietnamese cooperation and regional matters. A number of bilateral documents were signed following the international consultations.

A joint declaration on the results of the official visit by the General Secretary of the Central Committee of the Communist Party of Vietnam to the Russian Federation was signed.

21 September 2018. Reports: Vietnam's President Tran Dai Quang has died at age 61, after suffering from a "kind of highly virulent virus." Though he held one of the country's top four positions, and was officially the head of state, his role as president was seen as largely ceremonial. Rumors of his illness had circulated on social media for months, but there was no significant reaction in Vietnam.

Laos (Population. 6.8 M, rank 106, growth 1.5%. Not free: 12 of 100).

Cambodia (Population 16 M, rank 71, growth 1.5%. Not Free 31 of 100).

Mongolia (Population 3 M, rank 137, growth 1.6%. Free 85 of 100) 12 September 2018. Vladimir Putin had a meeting with Mongolian President Khaltmaagiin Battulga on the sidelines of the Eastern Economic Forum in Vladivostok, Russia.

Nepal: (Population 29.3 M, rank 48, growth 1.1%. Partly free 52 of 100).

Russia, Switzerland, Eastern Europe

Russia: (Population 143.9 M, rank 9, growth 0%. Not free: 20 of 100). 10 September 2018. Reports: Russia's ruble weakened to the lowest level since March 2016 on Monday, 10 Sep. The ruble dropped to Rbs70.115 per dollar (-0.2% on the day), in a sell-off fueled by concerns over the central bank's independence. Last week, prime minister Dmitry Medvedev called for rate cuts. The next interest rate decision is Friday, 14 Sep.

11 September 2018. Talks between Vladimir Putin and President of the People's Republic of China Xi Jinping have been held in Vladivostok.

The talks, which began in a restricted format and then continued with the participation of the two countries' delegations, covered bilateral cooperation and key international matters.

Following the talks, the two heads of state attended the ceremony for exchanging documents signed during the President of the People's Republic of China Xi Jinping's working visit to the Russian Federation. Among the documents signed were memorandums on establishing the Business Council of the Far East and the Baikal Region of Russia and North East of China and on consolidating Russian-Chinese regional, production and investment cooperation in the Far East, as well as a program for the development of Russia-China trade, economic and investment cooperation in Russia's Far East in 2018–2024.

Also signed were documents on cooperation between the Russian and Chinese Olympic committees and between Rossiya Segodnya International Information Agency and the China Media Group, as well as an agreement between Far Eastern Federal University and Chinese Academy of Social Sciences on establishing centers of Russian and Chinese studies. In addition, a loan agreement between Vnesheconombank and China Development Bank on granting up to 12 billion yuan and a treaty on the rights of the participants in the KAMAZ Weichai company were signed.

Vladimir Putin and Xi Jinping also made statements for the press.

President of Russia Vladimir Putin: President Xi, dear friend, Ladies and Gentlemen,

Allow me to begin by expressing my gratitude to President of China Xi Jinping for accepting our invitation to attend the Eastern Economic Forum in Vladivostok, for the first time as the main guest. President Xi is accompanied in Vladivostok by a large delegation, which includes senior government officials, representatives of regional governments and business leaders.

Tomorrow, President Xi and I, together with the President of Mongolia and prime ministers of Korea and Japan, will take part in the forum's plenary session. Today was President Xi's working visit to Russia. It included talks during which we discussed the most urgent bilateral and international matters, and outlined further plans to promote the comprehensive partnership and strategic cooperation between Russia and China.

As usual, we paid special attention to trade and economic cooperation. We noted with satisfaction that bilateral trade increased by almost one third in the first six months of the year, reaching $50 billion. We have every reason to believe that by the end of the year, trade will reach a record high of $100 billion.

The signing in May 2018 of the Agreement on Trade and Economic Cooperation between the EAEU and China creates additional opportunities for expanding bilateral trade flows.

Russia and China reaffirmed their interest in expanding the use of national currencies in bilateral deals, which would improve the stability of banking services during export and import transactions under the risky conditions on the global markets.

Energy is an important area of cooperation. Last year, Russia supplied 30 million tons of oil to China as part of intergovernmental agreements, or over 52 million tons when commercial deals are considered.

The construction of the Power of Siberia pipeline is being carried out as planned. The launch is scheduled for late 2019. Agreement has been reached on the main conditions for gas supply from the Far East. Chinese investors own a large share in the Yamal LNG project. Clients in 14 countries, including China, have received four million tons of liquefied natural gas from this enterprise since December 2017. China imports a large proportion of its electricity and coal from Russia. Russian-Chinese cooperation in the peaceful atom sphere is also developing. The first stage of the Tianwan Nuclear Power Plant is already in operation. This year, the third unit has been completed and the fourth is soon to be ready. Rosatom plans to build two more units there. We also note the expanding cooperation in science, in the peaceful use of nuclear energy. In addition, cooperation in agriculture is developing. Exports of Russian agricultural products to China increased by more than 50 percent during the first six months of this year: for example, 656,000 tons of grain were exported, more than during the whole of 2017.

We continue negotiations aimed at increasing the number of the Russian regions that can export wheat to China and at simplifying mutual supplies of meat and dairy products. We consider the strengthening of direct ties between Russian regions and Chinese provinces to be especially important. The 2018–2019 Years of Interregional Cooperation should promote this. President Xi Jinping and I will also meet with the participants of the roundtable discussion involving heads of Russian and Chinese regions.

Much work is being done by the Intergovernmental Commission for Cooperation and Development of the Far East and Baikal Region of Russia and Northeast China. The second meeting of the commission in Dalian in August focused on the expansion of the border infrastructure and international transport corridors.

Our humanitarian ties are multifaceted. The citizens of both countries show an increasing interest in mutual tourism. I must note that a record number of Chinese fans, about 70,000, visited the FIFA World Cup in Russia. Our cooperation in education, culture, sports, and youth exchanges is deepening.

We can see growing interaction between our countries in international organizations such as the UN, the Shanghai Cooperation Organization, BRICS, the G20, and others.

We will continue our joint efforts towards political and diplomatic settlement on the Korean Peninsula in accordance with the Russian-Chinese roadmap. We support the steps taken by the leadership of South and North Korea to restore bilateral relations and hope that the next inter-Korean summit in Pyongyang will be effective. We consider the normalization of relations between North Korea and the United States an important component in the overall stabilization process on the Korean Peninsula.

In conclusion, I would like to thank our Chinese friends for an informative and constructive dialogue. I am confident that these talks as well as numerous contacts at the Eastern Economic Forum will serve to further the development of friendly relations between our peoples and countries. Thank you.

President of the People's Republic of China Xi Jinping: President Putin, ladies and gentlemen, good afternoon.

I am very pleased to meet you together with my close friend President Putin. This is my seventh visit to Russia as President of China but it is the first time I take part in the Eastern Economic Forum. I was in Vladivostok eight years ago. This time I see a city that looks both familiar as well as new. I am sincerely happy that the city is developing dynamically. Today in the afternoon President Putin and I held sincere, deep and fruitful talks, discussed a wide range of matters related to bilateral relations and the topical international agenda and reached important agreements.

After this we continued our joint program: we have a roundtable discussion with the heads of Chinese and Russian regions planned. All these events are very important and representative; they show how wide and deep our cooperation is. Tomorrow President Putin and I will take part in the 4th Eastern Economic Forum where we will discuss cooperation and development plans with countries of the region. During the last four months President Putin and I have already had three meetings. This intensity of contacts proves the high level and special character of Russian-Chinese relations and stresses their priority in our foreign policy. Spanning over a period up until the close of the year President Putin and I have a number of other meetings scheduled which will take place at important events to continue our contacts.

The President and I agree that since the beginning of this year Russian-Chinese relations have been showing dynamic growth, have entered a new era of rapid development and are reaching a higher level. The parties reaffirmed firm mutual support in the choice of the development path that agrees with the national features of both countries as well as our security and development interests. All of this can serve as an example of what relations should be like between states and neighbor countries.

We are pleased to see that, step by step, joint efforts are turning the political advantages and strategic values of our bilateral relations into substantive results of cooperation. The bilateral trade grew to $58.3 billion during the first seven months of this year, which is 25.8 percent higher than during the same period last year.

Our trade is making progress. Both sides are actively working on the rapprochement of the projects One Belt, One Road and the EAEU, promoting large strategic projects in the energy sector, aviation, space and transport links and also developing our cooperation in new spheres, such as finance, agriculture, and e-commerce. Cooperation is impressive both in quantity and quality, it's being filled with new content and its borders are expanding.

We are developing our cultural and humanitarian cooperation. The ties between citizens of our countries are becoming increasingly closer. Records are being broken one after another when it comes to the number of student exchanges and tourists. We are particularly pleased to note the strengthening of the mutual understanding and friendship among young people.

The Ocean Russian Children's Centre in Vladivostok is the best example of love and friendship and demonstrates the true feelings of our young people. I am sure that this will build up the inexhaustible strength of friendship between China and Russia.

This and next years are years of interregional cooperation between China and Russia. A number of major events are being held in this connection. The regional cooperation mechanism in the formats Northeast of China – Russia's Far East and the Yangtze Volga rivers is developing. Contacts and cooperation between other regions of our countries are also growing. President Putin and I reaffirm our active support for comprehensive interregional cooperation and the establishment of twin ties between cities, provinces and regions, and all-round interregional cooperation for promoting friendship of our nations. I am sure that tomorrow's Eastern Economic Forum will give a fresh impetus to the deepening of interregional cooperation in the Far East as well as other areas. As permanent members of the UN Security Council and leading countries in the developing markets, China and Russia bear enormous responsibility for the maintenance of peace and stability together with the promotion of the development and prosperity all over the world.

We have similar or identical positions on international matters, broad common interests and firm foundations for cooperation. China-Russia cooperation in maintaining equality, justice, peace and stability throughout the entire world is gaining ever more importance against a backdrop of growing instability and unpredictability on a global scale.

Together with our Russian colleagues we will be promoting our fruitful cooperation in international affairs and step up our coordination at multilateral venues, such as the UN, SCO, and BRICS. In cooperation with the international community we will facilitate political settlement of urgent matters and hot spots and firmly uphold the goals and principles of the UN Charter. We will work together against the unilateral approach and trade protectionism, and for the creation of a new type of international relations and common destiny of humankind.

I would like to sincerely thank President Putin and our Russian friends once again for the warm and hospitable welcome accorded to the Chinese delegation during its visit to the Far East. I would also like to wish tomorrow's Eastern Economic Forum every success. Thank you.

President of Russia Vladimir Putin and President of China Xi Jinping visited the Far East Street exhibition held on the sidelines of the Eastern Economic Forum at Far Eastern Federal University.

12 September 2018. Reports: A day after Russia and China kicked off their largest ever war games, the two countries vowed to stand together against protectionism. "We see a serious challenge for all of the global economy, especially for the dynamically-growing Asia-Pacific, and its leadership," Vladimir Putin declared. Both countries are further looking into using national currencies in their transactions, sidelining the dollar.

History: In August 1968, a group of eight courageous people, including Pavel Litvinov, walked out on to the Red Square in Moscow to protest the Soviet invasion of Czechoslovakia. Their act of moral courage became a guiding light for Soviet dissidents, and post-Soviet protest leaders.

13 September 2018. Vladimir Putin and PRC President Xi Jinping visited a photo exhibition on the history of Russian-Chinese trade and economic cooperation. The exhibition is held on the sidelines of the Eastern Economic Forum in one of the buildings of the Far Eastern University.

The two leaders saw images depicting the key developments in bilateral trade, major strategic projects in the energy sector, aircraft manufacturing, inter-regional cooperation, as well as humanitarian and cultural ties. Vladimir Putin and Xi Jinping also watched a video clip on the history of the partnership between the two countries.

History: On October 1, the Russian Ground Forces mark 468 years since their foundation in 1550. This commemorative date was established in 2006, and refers to the anniversary of the Streltsy firearm infantry, the first regular troops in Russia.

Geneva, on Quai du Général Guisan (1874-1960), going southeast, Swissotel (center), Jardin Anglais (left), Place des Florentins (right).

Switzerland: (Population 8.4 M, rank 99, growth 0.9%. Free: 96 of 100).

Austria: (Population 8.7 M, rank 98, growth 0.3%. Free: 95 of 100).

Poland: (Population 38.1 M, rank 37, decrease 0.1%. Free: 89 of 100). Reports: Guided missile experts at the Raytheon Co. will provide Patriot surface-to-air missile systems for the government of Poland.

Croatia: (Population 4.1 M, rank 129, decrease 0.6%. Free: 87 of 100).

Finland: (Population 5.5 M, rank 116, growth 0.4%. Free: 100 of 100).

Romania (Population: 19.6 M, rank 59, decrease 0.5%. Free: 84 of 100)

Moldova: (Population: 4 M, rank 132, decrease 0.2%. Partly Free: 62 of 100).

Belarus: (Population: 9.4 M, rank 93, decrease 0.1%. Not Free: 20 of 100). 21 September 2018. At the Bocharov Ruchei residence in Sochi, Vladimir Putin met with President of the Republic of Belarus, Alexander Lukashenko, who is in Russia on a working visit.

Bulgaria: (Population: 7 M, rank 105, decrease 0.7%. Free: 80 of 100).

Slovenia: (Population: 2 M, rank 148, growth 0.1%. Free: 92 of 100).

Hungary: (Population: 9.7 M, rank 91, decrease 0.3%. Free: 76 of 100) 18 September 2018. In the Kremlin, Vladimir Putin met with Prime Minister of Hungary, Viktor Orban, who is in Russia on a working visit.
The agenda of the talks included key issues related to the further development of Russian-Hungarian cooperation, and a number of topical regional and international matters, in particular, the developments in Ukraine and Syria.

Ukraine: (Population: 44.2 M, rank 32, decrease 0.5%. Partly free: 61 of 100).

Latvia: (Population: 1.9 M, rank 150, decrease 1.1%. Free: 87 of 100).

Lithuania: (Population: 2.8 M, rank 141, decrease 0.6%. Free: 91 of 100).

Estonia: (Population: 1.3 M, rank 155, decrease 0.2%. Free: 94 of 100).

Serbia: (including Kosovo: Population: 8.7 M, rank 97, decrease 0.3%. Free: 76 of 100). 2 October 2018. Vladimir Putin met in the Kremlin with President of the Republic of Serbia, Aleksandar Vučić, who arrived in Russia on a working visit.

Kosovo ((Disputed: recognized by 110 countries, and not recognized by Serbia, Russia, and others) Population: 1.8 M, Partly free: 52 of 100).

Turkey: (Population 80.7 M, rank 19, growth 1.2%. Partly free: 38 of 100). 7 September 2018. Vladimir Putin had a meeting with President of Turkey, Recep Tayyip Erdogan, at the International Conference Centre in Tehran. The situation in the Syrian Arab Republic was the main topic of discussion.
Vladimir Putin and Recep Tayyip Erdogan arrived in the Islamic Republic of Iran to attend the summit of the heads of state, guarantors of the Astana process for facilitating the Syrian peace settlement.
17 September 2018. Vladimir Putin met with visiting President of the Republic of Turkey, Recep Tayyip Erdogan, at the Bocharov Ruchei residence in Sochi, Russia.
Following Russian-Turkish talks, Vladimir Putin and Recep Tayyip Erdogan made statements for the press.
The two heads of state witnessed the signing of the Memorandum of Understanding on Stabilization of the Situation in Idlib's De-escalation Zone by Russian Defense Minister Sergei Shoigu and Turkish Minister of National Defense Hulusi Akar.

Greece: (Population 11.1 M, rank 82, decrease 0.2%. Free: 84 of 100).

Republic of North Macedonia: (Population 2 M, rank 147, growth 0.1%. Partly Free: 57 of 100).

Albania: (Population 2.9 M, rank 139, growth 0.1%. Partly free: 68 of 100).

Cyprus: (Population 1.1 M, rank 159, growth 0.8%. Free: 94 of 100).

Kazakhstan (Population 18.2 M, rank 64, growth 1.2%. Not free: 22 of 100). 20 September 2018. Vladimir Putin had a telephone conversation with President of the Republic of Kazakhstan, Nursultan Nazarbayev, at Kazakhstan's initiative.

Armenia: (Population 2.9 M, rank 138, growth 0.2%. Partly free: 45 of 100). 8 September 2018. In the Kremlin, Vladimir Putin met with Prime Minister of the Republic of Armenia, Nikol Pashinyan, who is in Russia on a working visit.

Azerbaijan: (Population 9.8 M, rank 90, growth 1.1%. Not free 14 of 100). 27 September 2018. Vladimir Putin met with President of the Republic of Azerbaijan, Ilham Aliyev, in Baku.

Uzbekistan: (Population 31.9 M, rank 44, growth 1.5%. Not free: 3 of 100).

Kyrgyzstan (Population 6 M, rank 112, growth 1.5%. Partly free, 37 of 100).

Tajikistan: (Population 8.9 M, rank 96, growth 2.1%. Not free, 11 of 100). 28 Sep 2018. Vladimir Putin took part in the meeting of the CIS Heads of State Council in Dushanbe, Tajikistan. During the restricted format meeting the participants exchanged opinions on the current issues of the CIS. It was decided to pass on the CIS presidency 2019 to Turkmenistan, with the Republic of Tajikistan and the Republic of Uzbekistan acting as co-chairs.
The participants included President of Russia Vladimir Putin, Prime Minister of Armenia Nikol Pashinyan, President of Azerbaijan Ilham Aliyev, President of Belarus Alexander Lukashenko, President of Kazakhstan Nursultan Nazarbayev, President of

Kyrgyzstan Sooronbay Jeenbekov, President of Moldova Igor Dodon, President of Tajikistan Emomali Rahmon, Deputy Prime Minister of Turkmenistan Purli Agamyradov, President of Uzbekistan Shavkat Mirziyoyev, and Chairman of the CIS Executive Committee – Executive Secretary Sergei Lebedev.

Turkmenistan: (Population 5.7 M, rank 113, growth 1.7%. Not free, 4 of 100).

UK, Oxford: On Oriel Street, looking southeast to the west façade of Oriel College (1326), Merton St, Corpus Christy College (1517, right).

United Kingdom, Canada, South America

United Kingdom: (Population: 66.1 M, rank 21, growth 0.6%. Free: 95 of 100). 7 September 2018. Reports: As a result of cybercriminals' attacks, financial data have been stolen from 380,000 British Airways customers, who made online bookings in recent weeks. "The moment we found out... that's when we began an all-out immediate communication to our customers," CEO Alex Cruz told BBC Radio. Any customers who lose out financially from the cybercriminals' attacks will be compensated by the airline. People ask authorities to arrest the cybercriminals.

12 September 2018. Reports: A group of about 50 lawmakers in Theresa May's government, who oppose her proposals for a post-Brexit deal with the EU, have met to discuss how and when they could force her out of her job, the BBC reports. A leadership contest could ensue if 15% of Conservative lawmakers, currently 48, demand a vote of no confidence. Meanwhile, Bank of England Gov. Mark Carney has postponed his departure again - until 2020 - to help steer the U.K. economy past Brexit.

Ireland: (Population: 4.7 M, rank 123, growth 0.8%. Free: 96 of 100)

Canada: (Population: 36.6 M, rank 38, growth 0.9%. Free: 99 of 100). 5 September 2018. Reports: Senior officials from the U.S. and Canada are due to meet in Washington today in a bid to settle major NAFTA differences, amid pressure from the Trump administration. "No NAFTA is better than a bad NAFTA deal for Canadians and that's what we are going to stay with," Justin Trudeau told reporters, stating he would insist on keeping the Chapter 19 dispute-resolution mechanism, and existing protections that ban U.S. media firms from buying Canadian cultural industries.

14 September 2018. Reports: Canada is set to become the world's only major industrialized nation to legalize retail marijuana sales, starting Oct. 17, and the U.S. is taking contra-measures.

Mexico: (Population: 129.1 M, rank 10, growth 1.3%. Partly Free: 65 of 100).

Chile: (Population: 18 M, rank 65, growth 0.8%. Free 94 of 100).

Colombia: (Population: 49 M, rank 29, growth 0.8%. Partly free 64 of 100).

Argentina: (Population: 44.2 M, rank 31, growth, 1%. Free: 82 of 100). 20 September 2018. Reports: In Argentina GDP contracted 4.2% in Q2 of 2018. A drought at the beginning of the year reduced soybean and corn production, which account for a big part of exports, while more bad news followed suit. A selloff of the peso in May forced President Mauricio Macri to seek help from the IMF, as the government agreed to cut spending as part of a $50 B bailout.

Brazil (Population: 209.2 M, rank 6, growth 0.8%. Free, 79 of 100).

Peru: (Population: 32.1 M, rank 5, growth 1.2%. Free: 72 of 100)

Cuba: (Population: 11.4 M, rank 42, growth 0.1%. Not free, 15 of 100).

Bolivia: (Population: 11 M, rank 83, growth 1.5%. Partly free 68 of 100).

Paraguay: (Population: 6.8 M, rank 107, growth 1.3%. Partly free 64 of 100).

Panama: (Population: 4.1 M, rank 131, growth 1.6%. Free: 83 of 100).

Venezuela: (Population: 32 M, rank 43, growth 1.3%. Not free: 30 of 100). 14 September 2018. Reports: After a few weeks since the rollout of Venezuela's new money, which stripped five zeros off the bolivar, the inflation of the new currency is already 100%. That would push annual inflation above 100,000%, according to Bloomberg's inflation scale. It comes as Venezuela's Nicolas Maduro meets with President Xi of China, one of his ailing country's biggest creditors, which has reportedly agreed to extend a $5B credit line.

Nearly 2 M people have fled Venezuela's economic and political crisis since 2015, according to the U.N., which appealed for a "non-political" answer to an exodus that now numbers "some 5,000 people leaving Venezuela daily." Colombia, which has taken in more than a million Venezuelans, called last week for a response, saying the migrant crisis was biting into its GDP, and straining regional resources.

Guyana: (Population 777K, (rank 165, grows 0.6%). Free: 74 of 100).

Trinidad and Tobago: (Population 1.3 M, (rank 153, grows 0.3%). Free: 81 of 100).

Nicaragua: (Population 6.2 M, (rank 110, grows 1.1%). Partly Free: 47 of 100).

France, Germany, and neighbors

France: (Population 64.9 M, rank 22, growth 0.4%. Free: 90 of 100).

From Geneva to Mont Blanc (4810 m) on freeway A40, near Arâches la Frasse, with Mont Blanc (center back).

Belgium (Population 11.4 M, rank 80, growth 0.6%. Free: 95 of 100)

European Commission, European Union, EU: 28 EU countries: Austria, Belgium, Bulgaria, Croatia, Republic of Cyprus, Czech Republic, Denmark, Estonia, Finland, France, Germany, Greece, Hungary, Ireland, Italy, Latvia, Lithuania, Luxembourg, Malta, Netherlands, Poland, Portugal, Romania, Slovakia, Slovenia, Spain, Sweden and the UK.

25 September 2018. Reports: The EU will establish a special payment channel allowing companies to legally continue financial transactions with Iran without exposure to U.S. sanctions. The mechanism would facilitate payments related to Iranian oil trade,

exports, and imports. The details of the mechanism will come after future meetings with technical experts. The special purpose vehicle was jointly announced by EU foreign policy chief, and Iranian Foreign Minister, days ahead of the U.N. General Assembly, where Iran will be a key topic.

Germany: (Population 82.1 M, rank 16, growth 0.2%. Free: 95 of 100). 14 September2018. Reports: Volkswagen is halting production of its iconic Beetle next year, ending an 80-year run for a car that introduced many people to the German brand in the 1960s. It's the longest-lived and best-selling vehicles of all time, with 22.7 M sold worldwide.

Reports: Almost 64 millions of vehicles are currently registered in Germany, and the numbers are rising. And this increase in motorization can be observed on a global scale, too: According to some estimates, there could be about 1 billion cars in the world.

19 September2018. Vladimir Putin had a telephone conversation with Chancellor of the Federal Republic of Germany, Angela Merkel, at Germany's initiative.

The discussion focused on the Syrian settlement. The President of Russia informed the German Chancellor of the agreements between Russia and Turkey to promote stabilization in the Idlib de-escalation zone, reached at the September 17, 2018, talks with President of the Republic of Turkey Recep Tayyip Erdogan in Sochi.

The two leaders also reaffirmed their mutual commitment to further facilitating the settlement of the internal conflict in Ukraine, including as part of the Normandy Format. Vladimir Putin expressed his concern over the developments following the killing of DPR's head Alexander Zakharchenko, stressing the need to fully implement the 2015 Minsk Package of Measures, including a legislative recognition by Kiev of the region's special status.

In addition, Vladimir Putin and Angela Merkel discussed a number of matters related to overcoming negative trends on the global financial markets.

It was agreed to continue bilateral contacts at various levels.

Norway (Population 5.3 M, rank 118, growth 1%. Free: 100 of 100). Reports: U.S. Army officials are continuing their purchases of the M153 Common Remotely Operated Weapon Stations

(CROWS) II from Kongsberg Defense & Aerospace AS in Kongsberg, Norway, under terms of a contract announced Friday, 14 Sep.

Sweden (Population 9.9 M, rank 89, growth 0.7%. Free: 100 of 100). 10 September2018. Reports: Sweden's ruling center-left Social Democrats and Greens and their Left Party ally held 40.6% of the vote early Monday. The opposition center-right Alliance held 40.3%. The right Sweden Democrats came third with 17.6%, up 5% from four years ago.

The Netherlands (Population 17 M, rank 67, growth 0.3%. Free: 99 of 100).

Czech Republic (Population 10.6 M, rank 87, growth 0.1%. Free: 94 of 100).

Denmark (Population 5.7 M, rank 114, growth 0.4%. Free: 97 of 100).

Luxembourg (Population 583 K, rank 169, growth 1.3%. Free: 98 of 100).

Spain: (Population 46.3 M, rank 30, growth 0%. Free: 94 of 100). 6 September 2018. The President of Russia had a telephone conversation with Prime Minister of the Kingdom of Spain, Pedro Sanchez, at the latter's initiative. In the course of the discussion of the bilateral agenda, Vladimir Putin and Pedro Sanchez expressed an interest in further developing cooperation on the political, economic, cultural and humanitarian issues. They also covered the relations between Russia and the European Union.
The parties agreed to continue contacts at different levels.

Portugal: (Population 10.3 M, rank 88, decrease 0.4%. Free: 97 of 100).

India, Pakistan, Australia, and neighbors

India (Population: 1.3 B, rank 2nd, growth 1.1%. Free: 77 of 100). Reports: India is building a Monument for Chhatrapati Shivaji Maharaj (19 Feb 1630 – 3 April 1680, aged 50.1, King 1674 - 1680), with an equestrian statue of 120 m, and a total height of 210 m. Another monument will be the Statue of Unity, for Sardar Vallabhbhai Patel (31 Oct 1875 – 15 Dec 1950, aged 75.1), 182 m, plus the base 58 m – total 240 m, the World's tallest statue. The Statue of Liberty is 93 m.

Indonesia: (Population: 263.9 M, rank 4, growth 1.1%. Partly free: 65 of 100). 28 Sep 2018. Vladimir Putin sent a message of condolences to President of the Republic of Indonesia Joko Widodo in connection with numerous victims, and large-scale destruction, caused by a tsunami that struck the island of Sulawesi.

Australia: (Population: 24.4 M, rank 53, growth 1.3%. Free: 98 of 100). 5 September 2018. Reports: Australia's economy sped past all expectations in Q2 as rapid population growth fueled demand for homes and infrastructure, while bolstering consumer spending, despite slow wages growth. GDP was 3.4% higher than a year earlier, ahead even of the 2.9% growth boasted by the U.S., a remarkable feat given the nation's ever-changing procession of prime ministers.

New Zealand: (Population 4.7 M, rank 125, growth 1%. Free: 98 of 100).

Pakistan: (Population 212 M, rank 5, growth 2%. Partly free: 43 of 100

Philippines: (Population 104.9 M, rank 13, growth 1.5%. Partly free 63 of 100).

Singapore: (Population 5.7 M, rank 115, growth 1.5%. Partly free 51 of 100).

Thailand: (Population 69 M, rank 20, growth 0.3%. Not free 32 of 100).

Myanmar (Burma, Population 53.3 M, rank 26, growth 0.9%. Not free 32 of 100

Bangladesh (Population 164.6 M, rank 8, growth 1.1%. Partly free 47 of 100).
Sri Lanka (Population 20.8 M, rank 58, growth 0.4%. Partly free 56 of 100).
Malaysia (Population 31.6 M, rank 45, growth 1.34%. Partly free 44 of 100).
Brunei: (Population 428,000, rank 176, growth 1.3%. Not free 29 of 100).
Vanuatu: (Population 276,000, rank 185, growth 2.2%. Free 80 of 100)

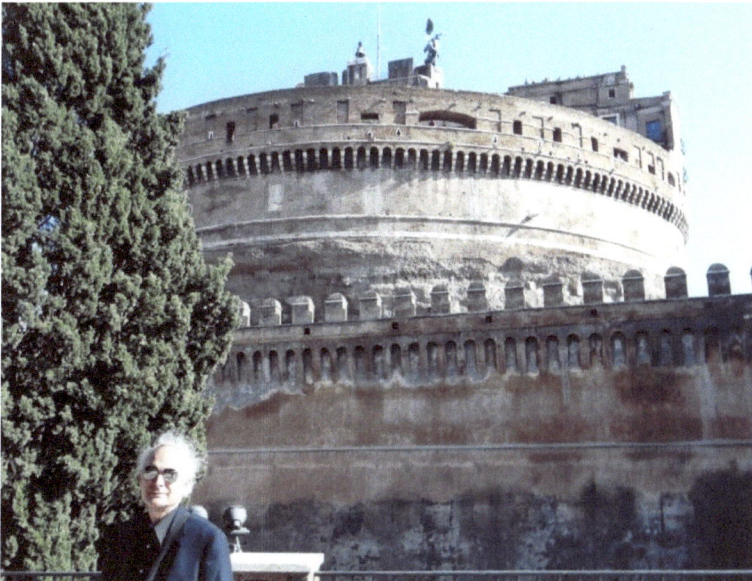

Roma: The west side of the Mausoleum (135-139) of Hadrian (76–138, Emperor 117-138, renamed Castel Sant'Angelo in 600), on Via Lungotevere Castello, seen from Viale G. Ceccarelli Ceccarius. Inside there is a huge spiral ramp (120 m) which ascends upwards the Mausoleum, to a terrace with a beautiful view of Rome.

Italy, Middle East, Africa

Italy: (Population 59.3 M, rank 23, decrease 0.1%. Free: 89 of 100). Reports: There is political turmoil in Italy, where the new anti-establishment government proposed a 2019 budget with a much wider deficit than the previous administration's target, setting up a clash with the European Commission. The government late Thursday, 27 Sep, night offered a budget with a deficit of 2.4% of GDP for the next three years, in a defeat for its economy minister, who had sought a deficit set as low as 1.6% next year, hoping to respect European Union demands that Italy progressively cut the fiscal gap to trim its debt. The full budget will be unveiled in October and will be scrutinized by the European Commission, which could reject it.

Vatican: (Population 792, rank 233 (last), decrease 1.1%).

San Marino: (Population 33,400, rank 218, growth 0.6%. Free 97 of 100)

Jordan (Population 9.7 M, rank 92, growth 2.6%. Partly free, 37 of 100).

Lebanon: (Population: 6 M, rank 111, growth 1.3%. Partly free: 44 of 100). History: Emir Farid Chehab (1908 – 1985, aged 77), was the chief of the Lebanese Sûreté Générale for 10 years, from 1948-1958, and a major figure in Lebanese politics and diplomacy for decades.

United Arab Emirates (UAE) (Population: 9.4 M, rank 94, growth 1.4%. Not free, 20 of 100).

Saudi Arabia (Population 32.9 M, rank 41, growth 2.1%. Not free: 10 of 100).

Yemen (Population 28.2 M, rank 50, growth 2.4%. Not free: 14 of 100).

Iraq (Population 38.2 M, rank 36, growth 2.9%. Not free: 27 of 100).

Iran: (Population 81.1 M, rank 18, growth 1.1%. Not free: 17 of 100. 7 September 2018. Vladimir Putin took part in the third trilateral meeting of the heads of state, guarantors of the Astana process for facilitating the Syrian peace settlement.
The Presidents of Russia, Iran and Turkey discussed issues related to long-term normalization of the situation in Syria, in particular, a set of additional measures to finally eradicate the stronghold of international terrorism, promote the political settlement process and solve humanitarian issues, including the creation of necessary conditions for the return of refugees and internally displaced persons. Following the summit, Vladimir Putin, Hassan Rouhani and Recep Tayyip Erdogan adopted a Joint Statement. They also gave a joint news conference.
After the Tripartite Summit of the guarantor states in the Astana process to promote the Syrian settlement, Vladimir Putin had a bilateral meeting with President of Iran Hassan Rouhani.
Towards the end of his visit to Iran, Vladimir Putin met with the country's Supreme Leader Ali Khamenei.
22 September 2018. Vladimir Putin sent his condolences to President of the Islamic Republic of Iran, Hassan Rouhani, over the tragic consequences of a terrorist attack in Ahvaz.

Israel: (Population 8.3 M, rank 100, growth 1.6%. Free: 80 of 100). 19 September 2018. Vladimir Putin had a telephone conversation with Israeli Prime Minister, Benjamin Netanyahu, at the initiative of the Israeli side. The Israeli Prime Minister expressed his condolences over the death of the 15 servicemen aboard the Il-20 aircraft shot down in Syria on September 17. With respect to a thorough investigation, Benjamin Netanyahu promised to provide detailed information on the activities of the Israeli Air Force over Syrian territory on that day, which will be delivered soon to Moscow by the Israeli Air Force commander.
Vladimir Putin noted that operations of this nature by the Israeli Air Force are in violation of Syria's sovereignty. In this particular case, Russian-Israeli agreements on preventing dangerous incidents had not been observed either, and that resulted in the Russian aircraft

coming under Syrian air defense fire. The Russian President called on the Israeli side to prevent such incidents in the future.

24 September 2018. Vladimir Putin had a telephone conversation with Prime Minister of the State of Israel, Benjamin Netanyahu, at the latter's initiative.

Palestine: (Population 4.9 M (rank 121, grows 2.7%). Not free: 28 of 100).

Egypt (Population 97.5 M (rank 14, grows 1.9%). Not free, 26 of 100).
League of Arab States (LAS) (22 countries: Algeria, Bahrein, Comoros, Djibouti, Egypt, Iraq, Jordan, Kuwait, Lebanon, Libya, Mauritania, Morocco, Oman, Palestine, Qatar, Saudi Arabia, Somalia, Sudan, Syria, Tunisia, United Arab Emirates and Yemen).

Qatar: (Population 2.6 M (rank 142, grows 2.7%). Not free: 26 of 100). Reports: The 15-month embargo of Qatar by Saudi Arabia and three other Arab nations has been a "blessing" for the gas-rich nation's economy. "If we lost around a 110 M market, we opened a 400 M market in countries including Turkey, Azerbaijan, Armenia, Pakistan, Iran and central Asia," the country's economy minister told Bloomberg. Since the boycott began, Qatari exports have risen 19%, while its global trade climbed 16%.

Kuwait: (Population 4.1 M (rank 130, grows 2.1%). Partly free: 36 of 100).

Oman: (Population 4.6 M (rank 127, grows 4.8%). Not free: 25 of 100)

Bahrain: (Population 1.5 M (rank 152, grows 4.7%). Not free: 12 of 100).

Syria: (Population 18.2 M (rank 63, decrease 0.9%). Not free: 0 of 100). 17 September 2018. Xinhua: Syria's air defenses responded to an Israeli attack near the international airport of the capital Damascus on Saturday, 15 Sep, evening, state TV reported.

The air defenses intercepted several missiles targeting the Damascus airport, said the report, citing a military statement.

The exact target of the attack is still unknown.

The attack is the latest in a string of Israeli missile strikes that targeted Syrian military bases during the protracted war in the country. On Sept. 4, Israeli warplanes infiltrated the Syrian airspace on a low altitude, targeting Syrian military sites in the central province of Hama, and the northwestern province of Tartus, according to the army. In July, Israel targeted again the scientific research center in the northwestern city of Masyaf.

The Saturday attack comes as the Syrian government is holding the Damascus international trade fair, not far from the airport.

Saturday is the last day of the week-long fair, where a large turnout thronged the fairground to enjoy the evening concerts.

The Israeli attack did not stop the concerts at the fairground.

24 September 2018. Vladimir Putin had a telephone conversation with President of the Syrian Arab Republic, Bashar al-Assad, at the latter's initiative.

Kenya: (Population 49.7 M (rank 28, growth 2.6%. Partly free, 51 of 100).

Libya: (Population 6.3 M, rank 109, growth 1.3%. Not free: 13 of 100).

Tunisia: (Population 11.5 M, rank 78, growth 1.1%. Free: 78 of 100).

Morocco: (Population 35.7 M, rank 39, growth 1.3%. Partly free: 41 of 100).

South Africa: (Population 56.7 M, rank 25, growth 1.3%. Free, 78 of 100).

Zimbabwe: (Population 16.5 M, rank 70, growth 2.4%. Partly Free, 32 of 100).

Sudan (Population 40.5 M, rank 35, growth 2.4%. Not Free: 6 of 100).

South Sudan (Population 12.5 M, rank 76, growth 2.8%. Not Free: 4 of 100)

Guinea: (Population 12.7 M, rank 75, growth 2.6%. Partly Free, 41 of 100).

Djibouti (Population 957,000, rank 160, growth 1.6%. Not Free: 26 of 100).

Somalia: (Population 14.7 M, rank 74, growth 3%. Not free: 5 of 100).

Niger (Population 21.4 M, rank 57, growth 3.9%. Partly free: 49 of 100).

Nigeria (Population 190.8 M, rank 7, growth 2.6%. Partly free: 50 of 100).

Cameroon (Population 24 M, rank 55, growth 2.6%. Not free: 24 of 100).

Sierra Leone: (Population 7.5 M (rank 103, grows 2.2%). Partly free: 66 of 100)

Chad: (Population 15 M (rank 73, grows 3.1%). Not free: 18 of 100).

The Gambia: (Population 2.1 M (rank 146, grows 3%). Not free: 20 of 100).

Malawi: (Population 18.6 M (rank 61, grows 2.9%). Partly free: 63 of 100).

Rwanda: (Population 12.2 M (rank 77, grows 2.4%). Not free: 24 of 100).

Burkina Faso: (Population 19.1 M (rank 60, grows 2.9%). Partly free: 63 of 100).

Central African Republic: (Population 4.6 M (rank 126, grows 1.4%). Not free: 10 of 100).

Senegal: (Population 15.8 M (rank 72, grows 2.8%). Free: 78 of 100).

Gabon: (Population 2 M (rank 149, grows 2.3%). Partly Free: 32 of 100).

Madagascar: (Population 25.5 M (rank 51, grows 2.7%). Partly Free: 56 of 100).

Democratic Republic of the Congo: (Population 81.3 M (rank 17, grows 3.3%). Not Free: 19 of 100). 7 September 2018. Reports: Congo has confirmed its first Ebola death in the eastern city of Butembo, the first urban outbreak of the virus. The current wave has already killed 89 people and it's close to becoming the eighth largest Ebola outbreak in history. A vaccination campaign has already been underway for weeks, with experimental treatments from companies like Merck and Gilead Sciences.

Angola: (Population 29.7 M (rank 46, grows 3.4%). Not Free: 24 of 100).

Zambia: (Population 17 M (rank 66, grows 3%). Partly Free: 56 of 100).

United Republic of Tanzania: (Population 57 M (rank 24, grows 3.1%). Partly Free: 58 of 100). Vladimir Putin sent a message of condolences to President of the United Republic of Tanzania, John Pombe Joseph Magufuli, over the tragic consequences of a passenger ferry capsizing on Lake Victoria.

Medical

People experience stress as they encounter changes in life. Long-term stress may contribute to or worsen other health problems, such as digestive disorders, headaches, and sleep disorders. Stress may worsen asthma and has been linked to depression, anxiety, and other mental illnesses.

The health joint venture formed by Amazon, Berkshire Hathaway, and JPMorgan has hired Jack Stoddard, most recently general manager for digital health at Comcast, as chief operating officer. Author and physician Atul Gawande started as CEO in July. The project was formed to deal with the problem of high healthcare costs for the three companies' combined 1.2 M workers.

30 more cases of illnesses linked to Salmonella contamination of Kellogg's Honey Smacks cereal have been reported, according to the CDC, bringing the total to 130 cases across 36 states. So far 34 people have been hospitalized, but no deaths have occurred. While Kellogg in June decided to recall 1.3 M boxes of Honey Smacks, the contaminated cereal is still being sold in some locations.

Eureka Therapeutics achieves regression of metastatic liver cancer using ET140202 T-Cell Therapy.

Beaumont Bio Med issues voluntary recall of all homeopathic aqueous/alcohol-based medicines.

7 September: National Grateful Patient Day: spreading gratitude and hope by thanking the doctors, nurses and their assistants who help the patients.

7 September 2018. Reports: All 250 people on separate American Airlines flights from Munich and Paris were "held for a medical review" on Thursday, 6 Sep, after arriving in Philadelphia from Europe. No one on either plane was quarantined, American Airlines said, but 12 people aboard became ill with flu-like

symptoms. The health scare comes a day after a similar outbreak aboard an Emirates flight from Dubai to New York.

Japan, Kobe (201 AD, the 5th largest city in Japan, 30 km west of Osaka): a Sogo store in Sannomiya Station (on Flower Road),

Scientists with the Virginia Tech Carilion Research Institute say a gene involved in the body's sleep cycle is a potential target for therapies to help patients with a deadly form of brain cancer known as glioblastoma. Scientific Reports

Patients with chronic lymphocytic leukemia (CLL), who feel more stress, also have more cancer cells in their blood, and elevated levels of three other markers of more advanced disease.
– Ohio State University, Cancer

In the U.S., prostate cancer is the second leading cause of cancer deaths in men (after lung cancer). The lower rate of prostate cancer seen in Asia has been attributed in part to soy being a staple food in most Asian diets. It's thought that isoflavone compounds in soy—which have been shown to accumulate in prostate tissue and act as weak hormones—may suppress cancer through both hormonal and non-hormonal mechanisms. For example, the isoflavone genistein preferentially binds to estrogen receptors in prostate tissue, and this may reduce growth of tumor cells and induce cell death.

When you consider the versatility, portability, affordability, and tastiness of the humble banana, it's not exactly shocking to see that global production of the tropical fruit is at an all-time high. In fact, bananas are the most exported fresh fruit in the world, according to the Food and Agriculture Organization of the United Nations.

FDA approved AstraZeneca's treatment for hairy cell leukemia

FDA approved subcutaneous formulation of Actemra for use in Active Systemic Juvenile Idiopathic Arthritis.

56% of parents of teens, who have sleep troubles, believe that the use of electronics is hurting their child's sleeping.
– Michigan Medicine - University of Michigan

The risks of alcohol consumption differ by the presence or absence of simultaneous use of other substances, the most common one being marijuana. Simultaneous alcohol and marijuana use may increase alcohol-related risks and societal costs. – Research Society on Alcoholism, Alcoholism: Clinical and Experimental Research

New data shows that the Archimedes virtual bronchoscopy navigation system significantly improves the diagnostic yield of lung cancer nodules located outside a patient's main airways.

Zika vaccine shows promise for treating deadly brain cancer.

BioLyte Laboratories issues voluntary recall of NeoRelief.

Vaccines play an important role in preventing and controlling the spread of infectious diseases. Common routes of administration include subcutaneous and intramuscular injections. These procedures not only require trained personnel, but may also cause pain or discomfort for the patient. Therefore, specialists work on a method for the delivery of enveloped viruses by oral vaccination, like taking a vaccination pill.

Merix Pharmaceutical's Cold Sore Treatment is now available in convenience stores.

Many consider that there is the 6th sense - the body maintaining its sense of balance.

European agency recommends Novartis' gene therapy for rare inherited disorder.

Researchers deploy new clinical trial regimen for glioblastoma.

An embargoed UCLA-led study suggests that an intensive, multifaceted online diabetes prevention program is as effective as in-person programs, and can make prevention programs more accessible to those at risk for developing diabetes.
– University of California, Los Angeles (UCLA), Health Sciences
American Journal of Preventive Medicine

Almost 16% of college students say they misuse prescription stimulants, often in the quest for better grades, a new survey of U.S. undergraduate, graduate and professional students has found.
– Ohio State University

In what Johns Hopkins Medicine researchers call an unusually comprehensive analysis of nationwide data, they conclude that the rate of lawnmower serious injuries persists at close to 6,400 a year, most of them requiring surgery and hospitalization, with high costs. – Johns Hopkins Medicine, Public Health Reports

Its name is an acronym used to convey its size, but researchers at Cornell Engineering and Weill Cornell Medicine are hoping their hand-held cancer detection device's impact in the developing world, where it proved effective in Uganda testing, will increase. – Cornell University
Nature Biomedical Engineering, Sept. 2018

In a study of 1,978 older adults, published Sept. 21 in the journal Scientific Reports, researchers at Duke Health and the Duke Clinical Research Institute found people with irregular sleep patterns weighed more, had higher blood sugar, and higher blood pressure. – Duke Health

A new auto-commentary looks at how an emerging area of artificial intelligence, specifically the analysis of small systems-of-interest specific datasets, can be used to improve drug development and personalized medicine.
– SLAS (Society for Laboratory Automation and Screening)

Newly published results of a study examining men with locally or regionally advanced prostate cancer show those treated with a radical prostatectomy, followed by radiation treatment, have a lower risk of death from prostate cancer, and improved overall survival outcomes, than those treated with radiation plus hormone therapy.
– Rutgers Cancer Institute of New Jersey, Cancer, Sept-2018

Astrazeneca's Imfinzi demonstrates significant overall survival benefit in unresectable, stage III lung cancer.

The healthcare industry continues to be plagued by cybercriminals' attacks. So far in 2018, 1.4 M records were opened in a cybercriminals' phishing attack on UnityPoint Health.
People ask authorities to arrest the cybercriminals.
October is National Cybersecurity Awareness Month.

To rapidly detect the presence of E. coli in drinking water, Cornell University food scientists now can employ a bacteriophage – a genetically engineered virus – in a test used in hard-to-reach areas around the world. The Royal Society of Chemistry, Aug. 2018

Biocompatible, Autoclave safe and EtO compatible constructed medical switches are making a difference in medical devices needing to meet sterilization demands.

The Food and Drug Administration approved Eli Lilly's Emgality injection for the preventive treatment of migraine in adults, one of three in a new class of drugs recently approved for migraines. LLY said it plans to sell the drug, known chemically as galcanezumab, at a list price of $6,900 per year, or $575 per month, identical to the list price for the other new migraine treatments, Aimovig from Amgen and Novartis, and Teva's Ajovy. Some 39 M Americans suffer from migraine headaches, according to the Migraine Research Foundation.

FDA approved a new drug for the preventive treatment of migraine.

Healthy older adults, who exercise regularly, are less likely to struggle for words on the tip of their tongue than older adults who aren't as fit.

FDA approved an antibacterial drug to treat serious lung disease using a new pathway.

Antares received FDA approval of testosterone replacement therapy.

Splitting up and getting back together is always hard to do, but for proteins, it's almost impossible. However, a computer-guided mathematical algorithm may help scientists find just the right spot to split a protein, and then reassemble it to functionality.
– Penn State College of Medicine, Nature Communications

Mathematics, Science & Artificial Intelligence (AI)

Toyota is recalling more than a million of its Prius and C-HR compact crossover vehicles globally, due to the risk of fire. If dust accumulates on the wire harness or the cover, the insulation on the wires could wear down over time, due to vehicle vibrations. This could cause an electrical short circuit, which could generate heat, and lead to a risk of fire.

Some types of birds, mostly storks, choose the high parts of MV and LV poles to build their nests during nesting season (January to April). Storks have been identified as responsible for shooting the lines, either because they touch the lines with the wings or because wood sticks or other materials fall from the nests that they build in the poles. Researcher are working to protect LV and MV distribution lines from bird collisions and nest formation.

Specialists are looking for new ideas for a formulation additive, or additives, that stabilizes the color of one of its formulated materials, preventing discoloration under exposure to sunlight and humidity.

Researchers are looking for a scalable synthetic route for the production of amphiphilic block copolymers, free of phosphorous- or sulfur-containing compounds and impurities, halides, or metals.

Researchers work on a project to develop artificial intelligence, machine autonomy, and cyber security programs for a future constellation of low-cost satellites operating in low-Earth orbit.

Specialists are working to create devices, which can provide direct current power for loads of up to 20 watts, to electronic instruments on rotating shafts for hydropower generating units.

Presently, no practical methods exist for continuously powering these instruments on a rotating shaft.

From delayed flights to power outages, ice buildup can cost consumers and companies billions of dollars every year in lost efficiency and mechanical breakdown. New research from Virginia Tech hopes to change that by using world's first passive anti-frosting surface, which fights ice with ice. – Virginia Tech
ACS Applied Materials & Interfaces

On 17 August 2017, only a couple of years after the first detection of gravitational waves from a binary black hole system, the Laser Interferometer Gravitational Wave Observatory (LIGO) observed gravitational waves from a new source: a binary neutron star system. Tens of telescopes, on the Earth and in space, followed-up the event, shedding light on some of the big mysteries of our Universe, from the origin of extremely energetic explosions in distant galaxies - the Gamma Ray Bursts - to the formation of heavy metals on Earth.

Computing researchers are working for new ways to apply artificial intelligence (AI) and machine learning to cyber security, in order to detect malware, and prevent it from infecting computers and data networks.

Mercury Systems Inc. in Andover, Mass., is introducing the EnsembleSeries LDS3517 embedded computing processing blade for advanced on-platform processing, machine learning, and artificial intelligence (AI) applications.

Sir Isaac Newton's laws of motion (Philosophiæ Naturalis Principia Mathematica (Mathematical Principles of Natural Philosophy), first published in 1687) have applications in the business world.

University of Florida scientists are finding that by covering new citrus trees with mesh, they can keep disease-carrying insects

from harming the plants. That could be a big step toward stemming the deadly citrus greening disease.
– University of Florida Institute of Food and Agricultural Sciences

Two separate studies show how researchers are using machine learning to train computers to spot and classify cells just by analyzing medical images.

Food sorting and grading are key food manufacturing processes, where optical sensing technologies help to ensure consistent quality and improve process efficiency.

Researchers are looking for new methods to quantitatively isolate an ashless dispersant, polyisobutylene succinimide, from engine oils.

Microphones can be now attached on the back teeth for invisible, hands-free radio secure communications.

Brain computer makes it possible to communicate telepathically with a drone swarm.

The addition of a new infrared camera at Argonne's Advanced Photon Source narrows the gap between basic and applied research in additive manufacturing.
– Argonne National Laboratory

The Penn State Department of Chemical Engineering's cutting-edge work in the nascent field of artificial water channels was the subject of a recent Faraday Discussions conference held by the Royal Society of Chemistry, and a breakthrough paper.
– Penn State College of Engineering, Nature Communications; Royal Society of Chemistry Faraday Discussion, June-2018

Specialists are seeking creative new ideas for a data visualization technique to manage and represent the most important metrics and data from online conversations.

Jeff Bezos' Blue Origin space transport company has won a contract to supply engines for the massive Vulcan rocket built by United Launch Alliance, the joint venture between Boeing and Lockheed Martin.

Silicon carbide has enjoyed renewed interest for its potential in quantum technology. Its ability to house optically excitable defects, called color centers, has made it a strong candidate material to become the building block of quantum computing.
– American Institute of Physics (AIP), Applied Physics Letters

Canadian Niagara Falls (8000 BC, Horseshoe Falls (left)), with the city Niagara Falls, Ontario, Canada, and its Skylon Tower (right, 1965, 160 m, a Revolving Dining Room, three outside mounted elevators, an observation deck at the tower's summit).

General news and issues

5 September 2018. Reports: When Jeff Bezos speaks about strategy and innovation, everybody should listen. An interview at *Forbes* with Amazon's CEO gives rare insight into how he does what he does.

5 September 2018. Reports: Amazon briefly joined yesterday the $1 T club. The e-commerce giant is so far up 75% in 2018, adding over $435 B in market cap - or about one Walmart. Analysts cite Amazon's ever-diversifying portfolio as a value driver, including the purchase of Whole Foods, last-mile deliveries, and its push into advertising.

"Painting is a music and a melody to be understood only by the intellect, and that with difficulty." - Michelangelo

Reports: Jeff Bezos wants to fix U. S. preschools.
At a rare public appearance in Washington by Jeff Bezos last week, the Amazon founder and CEO spoke on a variety of topics, including space, scheduling, and the importance of a good night's sleep in making key decisions.

Everyone knows that people's names should not ever be given to hurricanes and other disasters (one day they may want to name a hurricane "Washington") – but some bureaucrats don't care. These big storms should be named like Sep12-2018, Sep25-2000, Aug18-1970, Sep15-1961, Jan4-1951, May26-1908, Jun12-1887, etc. – in which case everybody would know exactly when the hurricane formatted. Giving a name just insults people, and does not help to date the hurricane. Also, it should be mentioned that a big hurricane brings over 4 B tones of water (if it would be taken from Lake Tahoe, its level would be 9 m lower).

There are right now practical technical methods to weaken, or even to stop hurricanes, which engineers could implement in several months, at a cost much less than the cost of the damages of just one big hurricane (over $120 B, not to mention fatalities, injured, and many other human sufferings) – but the bureaucrats and politicians don't care.

Life could be much better, if those in power would pay attention.

Age is truly nothing but a number, but the number is exactly related to time (which is the main force), therefore it is pure chronological. The attitude can, certainly, ameliorate the symptoms of the age, but cannot change the age.

Aphorism: "Your age is chronological, but your attitude can ameliorate its symptoms for a much better quality of life."

Tech giants spend $80 B to make sure no one else can compete.

The Facebook network was attacked by cybercriminals on Friday, 28 Sep, and this affects accounts of more than 50 M users – the cost is around $1.63 B.

People ask again the authorities to arrest the cybercriminals.

What all the people need now: healthier planet, healthier people, and a more innovative and computerized medical science (with more mathematical assistance).

Humor

A little sister was throwing out all her toys, and TV, and phone, etc.

The older sister asks:
- What are you doing?
- Throw out the old staff.
- Why?
- Mommy said that Maria is coming, and to prepare. Aunt Maria always brings us new presents.
- Stop it! They gave the name Maria to a hurricane!
- Tell them to call the hurricane with their aunt name, and let Aunt Maria to bring me presents!

A mother of a college student asks a professor:
- Why college students don't vote absentee?

The professor smiles:
- They don't know where to buy a postage stamp…..

A senior government official asks a small police clerk, who keeps track of tasks:
- What happens to police departments that collect more fines?

The clerk looks to the left and to the right, to make sure that nobody is around, and responds sotto voce:
- They solve fewer crimes.

Universe Axioms
Formulated by Michael M. Dediu

The following axioms are not independent of each other. They express in different ways the same concept of infinity.

Axiom 1. Pointing a theoretical laser from Earth, in any direction, at any time, after a finite amount of time the laser beam will touch an astronomic body.

Axiom 2. In any direction in space starting from Earth, at any time, there is an astronomic body from which the Earth can be theoretically seen.

Axiom 3. Infinity of space: Any straight line passing through the Earth's center intersects an infinite number of astronomic bodies.

Axiom 4. Infinity of time: Representing the time on a line, with the origin at the beginning of the year 1, the time goes to infinite in both positive and negative directions.

Axiom 5. Infinity of life: Because of the infinity of space and time, it is normal to consider that the life exists at any time, in an infinite number of places. Therefore right now, when you are reading this book, there is life outside the Earth, in an infinite number of places, but we do not know yet how to contact them.

Axiom 6. The Earth rotates itself around its polar axis, the Moon and many artificial satellites rotate around the Earth, in the Solar System all the planets and many other objects rotate around the Sun, the Solar System itself rotates around the center of the Milky Way galaxy, the Milky Way galaxy and all the billions of galaxies in our

Universe (denoted U_1) rotate around the center of our Universe U_1, our Universe U_1, together with billions of other similar Universes, are inside a bigger Universe U_2 and rotate around the center of U_2, then U_2 and many others like it are inside a bigger U_3 and rotate around the center of U_3, and so on. Therefore, in general, the Universe U_n together with many similar Universes are inside the bigger Universe U_{n+1} and rotate around the center of U_{n+1}, for any n natural number, which goes to infinity. This can be written in the formula:

$$U_1 \subset U_2 \subset U_3 \subset \ldots \subset U_n \subset U_{n+1} \subset \ldots, \text{ n natural number.}$$

UK, Oxford, Oriel College (1326, in the east range of First quadrangle, the ornate portico in the center, with the inscription Regnante Carolo).

Time Axioms

Formulated by Michael M. Dediu

Axiom 1. Time is the most important force in the Univers.

Axiom 2. Everything is a function of time.

Axiom 3. Time exists in absolutely everything.

Axiom 4. Time creates and distroys everything.

Axiom 5. Time is invisible, inodor, insipid, unpalpabil, unaudible, but exists evrywhere.

Axiom 6. There are infinitezimal time particles, without mass, which are present everywhere, and which actually continuously transform everything.

UK, Cambridge, From Trinity Lane looking south to the west part of the northern façade and entrance of King's College Chapel (1446).

Bibliography

"The Histories" by Polybius
"Discours de la Méthode" by René Descartes
"Meditationes de prima philosophia" by René Descartes
"Philosophiae Naturalis Principia Mathematica" by Isaac Newton
Chinese encyclopedia Gujin Tushu Jicheng (Imperial Encyclopedia)
"Encyclopédie" by Jean-Baptiste le Rond d'Alembert and Denis Diderot
"Encyclopaedia Britannica" by over 4,400 contributors
"Encyclopedia Americana" by Francis Lieber

Michael M. Dediu is also the author of these books (which can be found on Amazon.com, and www.derc.com):

1. Aphorisms and quotations – with examples and explanations
2. Axioms, aphorisms and quotations – with examples and explanations
3. 100 Great Personalities and their Quotations
4. Professor Petre P. Teodorescu – A Great Mathematician and Engineer
5. Professor Ioan Goia – A Dedicated Engineering Professor
6. Venice (Venezia) – a new perspective. A short presentation with photographs
7. La Serenissima (Venice) - a new photographic perspective. A short presentation with many photos
8. Grand Canal – Venice. A new photographic viewpoint. A short presentation with many photos
9. Piazza San Marco – Venice. A different photographic view. A short presentation with many photos
10. Roma (Rome) - La Città Eterna. A new photographic view. A short presentation with many photos
11. Why is Rome so Fascinating? A short presentation with many photos
12. Rome, Boston and Helsinki. A short photographic presentation
13. Rome and Tokyo – two captivating cities. A short photographic presentation
14. Beautiful Places on Earth – A new photographic presentation

15. From Niagara Falls to Mount Fuji via Rome - A novel photographic presentation
16. From the USA and Canada to Italy and Japan - A fresh photographic presentation
17. Paris – Why So Many Call This City Mon Amour - A lovely photographic presentation
18. The City of Light – Paris (La Ville-Lumière) - A kaleidoscopic photographic presentation
19. Paris (Lutetia Parisiorum) – the romance capital of the world - A kaleidoscopic photographic view
20. Paris and Tokyo – a joyful photographic presentation. With a preamble about the Universe
21. From USA to Japan via Canada – A cheerful photographic documentary
22. 200 Wonderful Places, In The Last 50 Years – A personal photographic documentary
23. Must see places in USA and Japan - A kaleidoscopic photographic documentary
24. Grandeurs of the World - A kaleidoscopic photographic documentary
25. Corneliu Leu – writer on the same wavelength as Mark Twain. An American viewpoint
26. From Berkeley to Pompeii via Rome – A kaleidoscopic photographic documentary
27. From America to Europe via Japan - A kaleidoscopic photographic documentary
28. Discover America and Japan - A photographic documentary
29. J. R. Lucas – philosopher on a creative parallel with Plato, An American viewpoint
30. From America to Switzerland via France - A photographic documentary
31. From Bretton Woods to New York via Cape Cod - A photographic documentary
32. Splendid Places on the Atlantic Coast of the U. S. A. - A photographic documentary
33. Fourteen nice Cities on three Continents - A photographic documentary
34. 17 Picturesque Cities on the World Map - A photographic documentary

35. Unforgettable Places from Four Continents, including Trump buildings - A photographic documentary

36. Dediu Newsletter, Volume 1, Number 1, 6 December 2016 – Monthly news, review, comments and suggestions for a better and wiser world

37. Dediu Newsletter, Volume 1, Number 2, 6 January 2017 (available also at www.derc.com).

38. Dediu Newsletter, Volume 1, Number 3, 6 February 2017 (available at www.derc.com).

39. London and Greenwich, - A photographic documentary

40. Dediu Newsletter, Volume 1, Number 4, 6 March 2017 (available also at www.derc.com).

41. Dediu Newsletter, Volume 1, Number 5, 6 April 2017 (available also at www.derc.com).

42. Dediu Newsletter, Volume 1, Number 6, 6 May 2017 (available also at www.derc.com).

43. Dediu Newsletter, Volume 1, Number 7, 6 June 2017 (available also at www.derc.com).

44. London, Oxford and Cambridge, A photographic documentary

45. Dediu Newsletter, Volume 1, Number 8, 6 July 2017 (available also at www.derc.com).

46. Dediu Newsletter, Volume 1, Number 9, 6 August 2017 (available also at www.derc.com).

47. Dediu Newsletter, Volume 1, Number 10, 6 September 2017 (available also at www.derc.com).

48. Three Great Professors: President Woodrow Wilson, Historian German Arciniegas, and Mathematician Gheorghe Vranceanu – A chronological and photographic documentary

49. Dediu Newsletter, Volume 1, Number 11, 6 October 2017 (available also at www.derc.com).

50. Dediu Newsletter, Volume 1, Number 12, 6 November 2017 (available also at www.derc.com).

51. Dediu Newsletter, Volume 2, Number 1 (13), 6 December 2017 (available also at www.derc.com).

52. Two Great Leaders: Augustus and George Washington - A chronological and photographic documentary

53. Dediu Newsletter, Volume 2, Number 2 (14), 6 January 2018 (available also at www.derc.com).

54. Newton, Benjamin Franklin, and Gauss, A chronological and photographic documentary
55. Dediu Newsletter, Volume 2, Number 3 (15), 6 February 2018 (available also at www.derc.com).
56. 2017: World Top Events, But Many Little Known, A chronological and photographic documentary
57. Dediu Newsletter, Volume 2, Number 4 (16), 6 March 2018 (available also at www.derc.com).
58. Vergilius, Horatius, Ovidius, and Shakespeare - A chronological and photographic documentary.
59. Dediu Newsletter, Volume 2, Number 5 (17), 6 April 2018 (available also at www.derc.com).
60. Dediu Newsletter, Volume 2, Number 6 (18), 6 May 2018 (available also at www.derc.com).
61. Vivaldi, Bach, Mozart, and Verdi - A chronological and photographic documentary.
62. Dediu Newsletter, Volume 2, Number 7 (19), 6 June 2018 (available also at www.derc.com).
63. Dediu Newsletter, Volume 2, Number 8 (20), 6 July 2018 (available also at www.derc.com).
64. Dediu Newsletter, Volume 2, Number 9 (21), 6 August 2018 (available also at www.derc.com).
65. World History, a new perspective - A chronological and photographic documentary.
66. World Humor History with over 100 Jokes, a new perspective - A chronological and photographic documentary
67. Dediu Newsletter, Volume 2, Number 10 (22), 6 September 2018 (available also at www.derc.com).

Mathematical research papers published in international mathematical journals

1. Dediu, M. On the lens spaces. *Rev. Roumaine Math. Pures Appl*. **14** (1969) 623-627.

2. Dediu, M. Sur quelques propriétés des espaces lenticulaires. (French) *Rev. Roumaine Math. Pures Appl.* **17** (1972), 871-874.

3. Vranceanu, G; Dediu, M. Tangent vector fields in projective spaces V_3 and in the lens spaces $L^3(3)$. (Romanian) Stud. Cerc. Mat. **24** (1972), 1585-1600.

4. Dediu, M. Tangent vector fields on lens spaces of dimension three (Italian) *Atti Accad. Naz. Lincei Rend. Cl. Sci. Fis. Mat. Natur.* **54** (1974), no. 2, 329-334 (1977

5. Dediu, M. Campi di vettori tangenti sullo spazio lenticolare $L^7(3)$. (Italian) *Atti Accad. Naz. Lincei Rend. Cl. Sci. Fis. Mat. Natur. (8)* **58** (1975), no. 1, 14-17.

6. Dediu, M. Tre campi di vettori tangenti indepedenti sugli spazi lenticolari di dimensione $4n+3$. (Italian) *Atti Accad. Naz. Lincei Rend. Cl. Sci. Fis. Mat. Natur. (8)* **58** (1975), no. 2, 174-178.

7. Dediu, M. Sopra la metrica Vranceanu generalizzata (Italian) *Atti Accad. Naz. Lincei Rend. Cl. Sci. Fis. Mat. Natur. (8)* **58** (1975), no.3, 354-359).

8. Dediu, M. Sopra la metrica Vranceanu generalizzata (Italian) *Atti Accad. Naz. Lincei Rend. Cl. Sci. Fis. Mat. Natur. (8)* **58** (1975), no.3, 354-359).

9. Dediu, S.; Dediu, M. Sopra gli spazi proiettivi. *Rend. Sem. Fac. Sci. Univ. Cagliari* **46** (1976), suppl., 149-152.

10. Dediu, M.; Caddeo, Renzo; Dediu Sofia Alcune proprietà di una superficie immersa in uno spazio di Hilbert. (Italian) *Rend. Ist. Mat. Univ. Trieste* **8** (1976), no. 2, 147-161 (1977)

11. Dediu, S.; Dediu, M.; Caddeo, R. Alcune proprietà della metrica di Vranceanu generalizzata. (Italian) *Rend Sem. Fac. Sci. Univ Cagliari* **46** (1976), suppl., 153-161.

12. Dediu, Sofia; Dediu, M.; Caddeo, Renzo The Vrănceanu metric in local coordinates. (Italian) *Atti Accad. Sci. Lett. Arti Palermo Parte I (4)* **37** (1977/78). 331-339 (1980)

13. Dediu, M.; Caddeo, Renzo; Dediu, Sofia The extension of an *E*-premanifold to an *E*-manifold. (Italian) *Rend. Circ. Mat. Palermo (2)* **27** (1978), no. 3, 353-358.

Chicago (Illinois, 1833, 2.7 million): Belmont Harbor (6 km north from downtown) on Lake Michigan (58,000 km^2, 494 km by 190 km, 176 m surface elevation, depth 281 m (max), 85 m (average)).

Michael M. Dediu is the editor of these books (also on Amazon.com, and www.derc.com):

1. Sophia Dediu: The life and its torrents – Ana. In Europe around 1920
2. Proceedings of the 4th International Conference "Advanced Composite Materials Engineering" COMAT 2012
3. Adolf Shvedchikov: I am an eternal child of spring – poems in English, Italian, French, German, Spanish and Russian
4. Adolf Shvedchikov: Life's Enigma – poems in English, Italian and Russian
5. Adolf Shvedchikov: Everyone wants to be HAPPY – poems in English, Spanish and Russian
6. Adolf Shvedchikov: My Life, My Love – poems in English, Italian and Russian
7. Adolf Shvedchikov: I am the gardener of love – poems in English and Russian
8. Adolf Shvedchikov: Amaretta di Saronno – poems in English and Russian
9. Adolf Shvedchikov: A Russian Rediscovers America
10. Adolf Shvedchikov: Parade of Life - poems in English and Russian
11. Adolf Shvedchikov: Overcoming Sorrow - poems in English and Russian
12. Sophia Dediu: Sophia meets Japan
13. Corneliu Leu: Roosevelt, Churchill, Stalin and Hitler: Their surprising role in Eastern Europe in 1944
14. Proceedings of the 5th International Conference "Computational Mechanics and Virtual Engineering" COMEC 2013
15. Georgeta Simion – Potanga: Beyond Imagination: A Thought-provoking novel inspired from mid-20th century events
16. Ana Dediu: The poetry of my life in Europe and The USA
17. Ana Dediu: The Four Graces
18. Proceedings of the 5th International Conference "Advanced Composite Materials Engineering" COMAT 2014
19. Sophia Dediu: Chocolate Cook Book: Is there such a thing as too much chocolate?

20. Sorin Vlase: Mechanical Identifiability in Automotive Engineering
21. Gabriel Dima: The Evolution of the Aerostructures – Concept and Technologies
22. Proceedings of the 6th International Conference "Computational Mechanics and Virtual Engineering" COMEC 2015
23. Sophia Dediu: Cook Book 1 A-B-C Common sense cooking
24. Sophia Dediu: Dim Sum Spring Festival
25. Ana Dediu and Sophia Dediu: Europe in 1985: A chronological and photographic documentary

USA, Rhode Island, Newport: St. Mary's Parish (1828, 1848-1852). President John F. Kennedy and Jacqueline Lee Bouvier were married here on Sep. 12, 1953.

www.ingramcontent.com/pod-product-compliance
Lightning Source LLC
Chambersburg PA
CBHW041714200326
41519CB00001B/158